Thomas William Conway

Compilation of the Laws of Louisiana Now in Force for the Organization and Support of a System of Public Education

Vol. 2

Thomas William Conway

Compilation of the Laws of Louisiana Now in Force for the Organization and Support of a System of Public Education
Vol. 2

ISBN/EAN: 9783337779481

Printed in Europe, USA, Canada, Australia, Japan

Cover: Foto ©Suzi / pixelio.de

More available books at **www.hansebooks.com**

COMPILATION

OF THE

LAWS OF LOUISIANA,

NOW IN FORCE,

For the Organization and Support of a System of

PUBLIC EDUCATION.

———•○•———

By THOMAS W. CONWAY,

SUPERINTENDENT OF PUBLIC EDUCATION.

———•●•———

As this life is a preparation for eternity, so is education a preparation for this life, and that education alone is valuable that answers these great primary objects.—*Bishop Short.*

———•●•———

NEW ORLEANS:
PRINTED AT THE OFFICE OF THE REPUBLICAN, 94 CAMP STREET.

1870.

Superintendents of Education.

———•♦•———

THOMAS W. CONWAY, State Superintendent of Education.

DIVISION SUPERINTENDENTS.

R. C. RICHARDSON, - - - - - First Division.

E. S. STODDARD, - - - - - - Second Division.

R. K. DIOSSY, - - - - - - - Third Division.

JAS. McCLEERY, - - - - - - Fourth Division.

R. C. WYLY, - - - - - - - Fifth Division.

J. B. CARTER, - - - - - - - Sixth Division.

CONTENTS OF COMPILATION.

——•••——

CONTENTS OF APPENDIX.

INTRODUCTION.

Special attention of all officers charged with the execution of the provisions of these laws, and all teachers and heads of families generally, is invited to this compilation. All existing provisions of these laws, that are now in operation in the State, have been carefully preserved in the text, and, to avoid confusion and misconception, care has been taken to exclude therefrom all sections, paragraphs and clauses of the statutes that have been modified or repealed by subsequent enactments.

In this compilation appear the "Act to Regulate Public Education in the State of Louisiana, and to raise Revenue for the support of the same," No. 6 of extra session of 1870, and all antecedent acts and parts of acts not repealed thereby; to all of which ready reference can be had by consulting the accompanying Contents.

In the Appendix will be found title vii. of the Constitution of 1868, relating to Public Education, on which the provisions of Act No. 6, extra session of 1870, are founded; also, a brief abstract of such provisions of the laws as relate to the creation, preservation and present condition of the respective School Funds in the State Treasury; a complete text of the law, as now in force, for the government of the State Seminary of Learning and Military Academy, with reference to the act relative to the University of Louisiana; and a memoranda of the amount appropriated by the State since 1866, for the promotion of education.

The "Act (of the United States Congress) to establish a Department of Education," approved March 10, 1867, will also be found in the Appendix, with copy of circular letter issued by the Commissioner of Education, and a "Schedule of information sought respecting Systems, Institutions, and Agencies of Education."

Division Superintendents will see that a copy of this pamphlet is placed in the hands of all persons above enumerated; and Secretaries of District Boards will make it their especial care to furnish, in their periodical reports as required by law, complete and accurate statements of all such matters as come within their districts. If, in any instance, positive statistics and facts cannot be obtained, estimated reports will be given by the Secretaries, according to their best available means of information.

The cordial aid and co-operation of School Officers, Supervisors, and Teachers of Educational Institutions, and all other good citizens desirous of seeing the State of Louisiana ranked in intellectual advantages, beside any of her sister commonwealths, are earnestly solicited to thus vindicate her honor and dignity.

All necessary information for the promotion of this object not contained in this pamphlet, will be promptly furnished, on receipt of communications, by the Compiler.

THOMAS W. CONWAY,
Superintendent of Public Education.

AN ACT

TO

REGULATE PUBLIC EDUCATION

IN THE STATE OF LOUISIANA,

AND TO RAISE REVENUE FOR THE SUPPORT OF THE SAME.
APPROVED MARCH 16. 1870, WITH INDEX THERETO.

PREPARED BY

THOMAS W. CONWAY,

SUPERINTENDENT OF PUBLIC EDUCATION.

To which is appended Rules and Regulations for the Government of the Schools,
by the State Board of Education.

SPECIAL NOTICE.

A copy of this pamphlet will be furnished to each member of the State Board of Education, each Division Superintendent, each District Board of School Directors, the President or clerk of each Police Jury, to Parish Treasurers and State Tax Collectors, District Attorneys, and all other officers and citizens needing information as to the school laws, who should preserve them for reference.

The Division Superintendents are especially charged with the distribution of these pamphlets throughout their respective divisions. Such persons as need copies and are not furnished with the same before the first day of August next, are requested to address their proper Division Superintendent, or this office, and they will be promptly supplied.

THOS. W. CONWAY,
State Superintendent of Public Education.

New Orleans, May 15, 1870.

AN ACT

TO

REGULATE PUBLIC EDUCATION

IN THE

STATE OF LOUISIANA AND CITY OF NEW ORLEANS, AND
TO RAISE A REVENUE FOR THAT PURPOSE.

SECTION 1. *Be it enacted by the Senate and House of Representatives of the State of Louisiana, in General Assembly convened,* That the common schools of the State, and such High and Normal schools as may be established and maintained by the State, shall be under the management of a State Board of Education, which shall consist of the Superintendent of Public Education and of six members, to be appointed as is hereinafter provided.

Board of Education.

SEC. 2. *Be it further enacted, etc.,* That for the purpose of regulating public education in free schools, the State shall be divided into six divisions. All that part of the First Congressional District outside of the city of New Orleans shall form the First Division. All that part of the Second Congressional District outside of the city of New Orleans shall form the Second Division. The Third, Fourth and Fifth Congressional Districts shall form the Third, Fourth and Fifth Divisions, and the city of New Orleans shall constitute the Sixth Division, to be known as the Division of New Orleans.

School Divisions

SEC. 3. *Be it further enacted, etc.,* That immediately upon the passage of this act, the Governor shall, on the nomination of the State Superintendent of Education, appoint by and with the advice and consent of the Sen-

Nomination and appointment of Division Superintendents.

ate, one Division Superintendent for each of the Divisions hereinbefore named, said person to be a resident of the division for which he is appointed. The Division Superintendents so appointed and chosen shall take the oath required by State officers, and shall hold their offices for three years, and until their successors are duly appointed or chosen and qualified. The Division Superintendent for the city of New Orleans shall receive a salary of two thousand five hundred dollars ($2500) per annum, and each other Division Superintendent shall each receive a salary of two thousand five hundred dollars ($2500) per annum, payable quarterly by the State Treasurer, out of the public school fund, upon his own warrant.

Salaries.

Sec. 4. *Be it further enacted, etc.*, That the six Division Superintendents shall, with the Superintendent of Education, constitute a State Board of Education. The State Superintendent shall be *ex officio* president of the board, and its executive officer. The board so constituted shall hold one regular annual meeting in New Orleans, at the office of the Superintendent of Public Education, commencing the first Monday in January. The Superintendent of Public Education may call special meetings upon the written request of any five members.

Superintendent president of board.

Sec. 5. *Be it further enacted, etc.*, That the State Board of Education, so constituted and organized, shall have the power to recommend a uniform series of text books, and shall make all needful rules and regulations for the government of the public schools throughout the State, subject to the provisions of this act. It shall be the duty of said Board of Education to make a general regulation whereby all schools established under this law, shall be, according to the provisions of the constitution, open to all children of this State between the ages of six and twenty-one years, without distinction of race, color or previous condition, and in case of failing to pass such regulations, the members of said board shall forfeit the salary allowed them. A majority of the board shall form a quorum. The board is hereby constituted a body corporate and politic in law, with power to sue and be sued.

Powers and duties.

Quorum.

The president of the board shall be the officer upon whom citation or legal process may be served. The board may employ counsel.

DIVISION SUPERINTENDENTS.

Sec. 6. *Be it further enacted, etc.*, That the Division Superintendents shall have general supervision of all public schools within their respective divisions, subject to all rules and regulations passed by the State Board of Education. They shall examine and certify to the qualifications of all applicants to teach within their respective divisions, as hereinafter provided, unless such applicants hold a certificate of qualification from the State Superintendent. They shall receive and transmit all reports from the Board of School Directors to the State Superintendent. *[Powers of Division Superintendents.]*

Sec. 7. *Be it further enacted, etc.*, That the Division Superintendent shall, once in each three months, at such place as he may designate in his division, not to be a less number than one [for] each two parishes, meet all those who are desirous of passing an examination, and for the transaction of all other business within his jurisdiction, in some suitable room at the seat of justice of the parish, or at any other place, as occasion may require, and shall notify the parish judge of the place of meeting. *[Duties.]*

Sec. 8. *Be it further enacted, etc.*, That the Division Superintendent may revoke the certificate of any teacher in the parish for any reasons which would have justified the withholding thereof when the same was given. And the Board of School Directors, upon sufficient cause shown, may dismiss any teacher from any school in the district. *[May revoke certificates.]*

Sec. 9. *Be it farther enacted, etc.*, That on or before the fifth day of October in each year, he shall make a report to the State Board of Education, containing a digest of the reports to him by the Secretaries of the District Boards, and such other matters as he shall be directed to report by the said Secretary, and such as he *[Reports.]*

himself may think pertinent and material, and especially such as will show the condition of the schools under his charge. He shall also suggest such improvements in the system as he may think judicious. He shall also, by the fifth day of October in each year, file with the Recorder of the parish an abstract of the number of youths between the ages of six and twenty-one years, residing in each ward and school district within his parish.

Should he fail to make either of the reports required in this section, he shall forfeit to the school fund of his district the sum of fifty dollars, and shall, besides, be liable for all damages caused by such neglect.

SEC. 10. *Be it further enacted. etc.*, That he shall at all times conform to the instructions of the State Board of Education as to matters within their jurisdiction. He shall serve as the organ of communication between the State Board of Education and the Superintendent of Public Education and District Board of School Directors. He shall transmit to the District Board of School Directors or teachers all blanks, circulars and other communications which are to them directed, and shall entertain and decide all appeals taken from the decisions of District Boards of School Directors.

He shall organize and conduct, once in each year, for his own division, at such times as, after conference with the Superintendent of Public Education, may be designated, a teachers' institute, at some central locality in the division, to which access is convenient, and where the teachers will receive the encouragement of hospitality.

In this work the Superintendent will be aided by a professor from the Normal school, or by some practical teacher appointed by the State Superintendent.

He shall also encourage and assist at teachers' associations, to be convened four times each year, if practicable, on the last Saturday of some month in each quarter, in each parish or in several parishes united, urging the attendance of the teachers of the same, for the purpose of mutual conference and instruction in their duties.

He shall also report the number of private schools, academies and colleges in the division; number of pupils, male and female; and all other information, in such form as the State Superintendent may prescribe, so as to present a full view of their educational facilities. Reports of private schools.

He shall perform such duties and make such reports, in addition to those required in this act, as the State Board of Education may determine.

SUPERINTENDENT OF PUBLIC EDUCATION.

Sec. 11. *Be it further enacted, etc.*, That an office shall be provided for the Superintendent of Public Education at the seat of government, and to cost not more than eight hundred dollars per year (payable out of the public school fund on his own warrant), in which he shall file all papers, reports and public documents transmitted to him by the Division Superintendents of the several divisions, and by boards of directors, each year separately, and hold the same in readiness to be exhibited to the Governor, or to a committee from either house of the General Assembly, at any time when required, and shall require to be kept a fair record of all matters pertaining to his office. Office of Superintendent.

Sec. 12. *Be it further enacted, etc.*, That he shall make a report to the General Assembly at each session thereof, which shall embrace— Reports of school children.

First—A statement of the condition of the public schools throughout the State, the number of scholars attending in the various parishes and towns between the ages of six and twenty-one years, and the condition of the public school libraries.

Second—A statement of all rules and regulations adopted by the State Board, and whatever suggestions he may deem it expedient to offer upon the efficient working of this law. Of rules.

Sec. 13. *Be it further enacted, etc.*, That the Superintendent of Public Education shall appoint a secretary, and shall prescribe the duties of his office, not inconsistent with this act. He shall receive for his salary the sum of three thousand dollars ($3000) per annum, pay- Secretary of the State Superintendent.

able in monthly installments out of the public school funds, by the Treasurer of the State, upon the warrant of the Superintendent of Public Education. He will take the usual oath of office.

Sec. 14. *Be it further enacted, etc.,* That the Superintendent of Public Education shall be charged with the general supervision of all the Division Superintendents, and all the common, high or normal schools of the State; and he shall see that the school system is, as early as practicable, carried into effect, and put in uniform operation. With a general view to these special duties, he shall meet the Division Superintendents at least once in each year, in each division, at such time and place as he may appoint, giving due notice of such meeting; and it is hereby made the duty of the said Division Superintendents to attend each meeting, the object of which shall be to accumulate valuable facts relative to common schools, to compare views, discuss principles, and in general to listen to all communications and suggestions, and to enter in all discussions relative to the compensation of teachers, their qualifications, branches taught, method of instruction, text books, division libraries, apparatus, and all other matters embraced in the common school system. He shall visit such schools as he may have it in his power to do, and witness the manner in which they are conducted. His traveling expenses incurred in such visit shall be paid by the State Treasurer out of the public school fund upon his warrant; *provided,* That the same shall not exceed the sum of one thousand dollars in any one year. The Superintendent of Public Education shall cause as many copies of this act, and all other school acts in force, with the forms, regulations and instructions herein contemplated thereto annexed, to be from time to time printed and distributed among the Division Superintendents, as he shall deem expedient, directing the latter to distribute the same among the several school divisions of the State. He shall also prepare, and cause to be distributed to the several Division Superintendents, a form of certificate in blank, to be granted to teachers; also, all other blank

Marginal notes:

General supervision.

Superintendent to meet the Division Superintendents.

Traveling expenses.

Distribution of School documents.

forms necessary to be used in carrying out this act and
all other acts. He shall, annually, on the first day of Report to the Auditor.
January, report to the Auditor of Public Accounts the
number of persons in each parish of the State between
the ages of six and twenty-one years. He shall make a To General Assembly.
report to the General Assembly and the State Board of
Education at each session thereof, which shall embrace —
· *First*—A statement of the condition of the common
school divisions therein, the number of schools in the Statement of Schools and Scholars.
State, the number of scholars between six and twenty-one
years of age, and also the number in each parish who
have attended school the previous year, as returned by
the several Division Superintendents, the number of books
in the division libraries, and the value of all apparatus in
the schools.

Second—Such plans as he may have matured for the
management and improvement of the common school Plans.
fund, and for the better and more perfect organization
and efficiency of common schools.

Third—All such matters and things relating to his
office, and to the common schools, as he shall deem expe- Other matters.
dient to communicate.

Fourth—He shall cause his report to be printed, and
shall present five hundred copies thereof to each body on Printed report.
or before the second day of their session, for distribution.

Sec. 15. *Be it further enacted, etc.*, That whenever
reasonable assurance shall be given by the Division Su- Teachers' Institute.
perintendent of any division to the Superintendent of
Public Education, that a number of not less than thirty
teachers desire to assemble for the purpose of holding a
teachers' institute in said division, to remain in session
for a period of not less than six working days, he shall
appoint such time and place for said meeting, and such
lectures as the said teachers shall suggest, and shall give
due notice thereof; and for the purpose of defraying the
expenses of said institutes, there is hereby appropriated,
out of any moneys in the State treasury not otherwise
appropriated, a sum not exceeding fifty dollars annually,
for one such institute in each division held as aforesaid,

which the said Superintendent of Public Education shall immediately transmit to the Division Superintendent in whose division the institute shall be held, who shall pay out the same as the institute shall direct, provided, that a like sum shall be contributed by the division.

Sec. 16. *Be it further enacted, etc.*, That the State Board of Education shall appoint for each incorporated city or town in the State, except in the city of New Orleans, a Board of School Directors of not less than three nor more than five members, who shall exercise all the powers and duties herein conferred upon District Boards of Directors, and shall hold their offices for two years, and until their successors shall be duly elected and qualified according to law.

Sec. 17. *Be it further enacted, etc.*, That the board appointed for the town of Algiers shall control public schools in the parish of Orleans, not within the limit of the city of New Orleans. There shall be a board appointed for that part of the parish of Jefferson on the right bank of the Mississippi river. There shall be a board appointed for the parish of Jefferson on the left bank. Should any part of the said territory be hereafter incorporated within the city of New Orleans, said board shall have control over all territory remaining out of the limits of New Orleans, and the board for the city of New Orleans shall control all schools within the territory thus brought within the limits of the city of New Orleans: said boards of Algiers and Jefferson shall have the powers and duties of, and be governed by the regulation herein provided for District Boards of School Directors in other parishes.

Sec. 18. *Be it further enacted, etc.*, That the State Board shall appoint for each parish in the State, except the parishes of Orleans and Jefferson, a board of school directors, consisting of five or more persons, who shall be chosen, when practicable, from the several jury wards of the parish.

Sec. 19. *Be it further enacted, etc.*, That the members of the boards of school directors shall hold office for

Appointment of School Directors

School Board of Algiers.

Jefferson.

Provision for incorporation with New Orleans.

Appointment of parish boards

Term of office.

two years, and until their successors are appointed and
qualified. The term of office of the directors appointed
under this law shall begin on the first day of May, 1870,
after the approval of the same, but they shall be appointed and shall assume the duties of their office immediately
upon the passage of this act. They shall take the oath Oath of office
of office, which shall be filed with the Superintendent of
Public Education.

SEC. 20. *Be it further enacted, etc.*, That each Board
of School Directors hereinbefore provided for is hereby Incorporation of School Boards.
constituted a body corporate and politic in law, with
powers to sue and be sued. The body shall be known
and styled "The Board of School Directors of the town,
city or parish of ——," as the case may be. The
President of the Board shall be the officer upon whom
citation may be served.

SEC. 21. *Be it further enacted, etc.*, That the powers
and duties of each Board of School Directors hereinbe- Powers and duties.
fore provided for, shall be as follows:

First—To elect from among their members a president, Officers.
secretary and treasurer.

The treasurer shall give bonds in an amount not less
than five thousand dollars, to be approved by the parish Treasurer bond.
or district judge and the recorder of the parish, and a
copy thereof to be forwarded to the Superintendent of
Public Education, for the faithful performance of his
duties under this act. Said bond may, from time to time,
be increased by the order of the board or of the district
judge, in proportion to the amount of school funds in the
hands of the treasurer. The board shall, from time to
time, examine the accounts of the treasurer and settle
them.

Second—To appoint for each ward school district in
their parish a board of three district school directors. District direct-
Said district school directors shall hold their office for ors,
two years from the time of their appointment, and until
their successors are duly elected or appointed and
qualified.

Third—To visit and examine the schools of the several districts of the parish, from time to time, and to meet and advise with the several boards of district school directors as occasion may require.

Fourth—To report to the State Board of Education, and to the Superintendent of Public Education, all deficiencies in the schools, or neglect of duty on the part of teachers, directors, division superintendents or other officers.

Fifth—To receive from the State tax collector all proceeds of any parish school tax levied by the police jury in accordance with this law, and to apportion the same among the several ward school districts of their parish in proportion to the number of persons in their district, between the ages of six and twenty-one years.

Sixth—To make such needful by-laws and regulations for their own government, not inconsistent with this law, as they may deem proper.

The treasurer of the board shall receive all money on account of the board, and pay out the same on warrants signed by the president and countersigned by the secretary, and he shall keep a correct account of all expenses and receipts in books provided for that purpose, which shall always be open for inspection.

He shall render a monthly report to the board, and an annual report to the division superintendent, on or before the tenth day of January.

DUTIES OF OFFICERS OF SCHOOL BOARD.

SEC. 22. *Be it further enacted, etc.*, That each police jury or other ward that is now, or may be hereafter organized in the parishes of this State, is hereby declared a school district for all the purposes of this act. That the District Board of School Directors of each school district, which is now or may hereafter be organized in the State, is hereby made a body corporate by the name of the "Ward District of ———, in the parish of ———, and State of Louisiana," and in that name may hold property, become a party to suits and contracts, and do other corporate acts. That the District Board of School Directors shall hold their regular meetings on the first Saturday after the first Monday in April and October in each year, and may hold such special and adjourned meetings as occasion may require. They shall organize by electing from their own number a president, treasurer and secretary. That the duties of the directors shall be as follows:

First—To make all contracts, purchases, payments and sales necessary to carry out any vote of the district; *Provided*, That before erecting any school house they shall consult with the Superintendent of Public Education as to the most approved plan for such building.

Second—To admit pupils not belonging to the district, as provided for in section twenty-five of this act, to their schools, on such terms as they may agree upon.

Third—To determine the number of schools which shall be established, and the length of time each shall be taught, subject to the provisions of section twenty-three of this act.

Fourth—To fix the site for each school house, taking into consideration the wants and necessities of the people of each portion of the district.

Fifth—To establish graded or union schools wherever they may be necessary; and they may, as occasion re- quires, select a person who shall have the general super- vision of the schools in their districts, subject to rules and regulations of the board.

Sixth—To determine what branches shall be taught in the schools of their district.

Seventh—To require the secretary and treasurer each to give bond to the district in such penalty, and with such sureties as they may determine upon, conditioned for the faithful performance of their duties under this act. The bond shall be filed with the president of the board, and a copy of the same shall be sent to the Superintendent of Public Education, and in case of breach of condition thereof, he shall bring suit thereon in the name of the district.

Eighth—They shall, from time to time, examine the accounts of the treasurer, and make settlement with him, and present at each regular meeting of the election a full statement of the receipts and expenditures of the district, and all matters delegated to them to perform, and all such other matters as may be deemed important.

Ninth—To visit the schools in their district, and aid the teachers in establishing and enforcing rules for the government of the schools, and see that they keep a correct list of the pupils, embracing the period of time during which they attend school, the branches taught, and such other matters as may be required by the division superintendent.. A majority of the board shall be a quorum to transact business, but a less number may adjourn from time to time.

Each district board shall adopt a uniform series of books for all the schools in their district, and such series shall not be changed oftener than once in two years.

DUTIES OF DISTRICT OFFICERS.

SEC. 23. *Be it further enacted, etc.*, That the president shall preside in all meetings of the board and of the district; shall draw all drafts upon the State Treasurer and upon the treasurer of the parish board for money apportioned to his district; sign all orders on the district treasury, specifying in the order the fund on which they are drawn, and the use for which the money is assigned; and he shall sign all contracts. The president shall appear in behalf of his district in all suits brought by or against the same, but when he is individually a party, this duty shall be performed by the secretary; and in all cases where suits may be instituted by or against any of the school officers, to enforce any of the provisions herein contained, counsel may be employed by the Board of Directors. The secretary shall record all the proceedings of the board and district meetings in separate books kept for that purpose; shall preserve copies of all reports made to the State and Division Superintendents; shall file all papers transmitted to them pertaining to the business of the district, and shall countersign all drafts, warrants and orders drawn by the president. He shall keep an accurate account of all the expenses incurred by the district, and shall present the same to the Board of Directors, to be

Marginal notes:
Regulating schools.
Quorum.
Uniform text books.
President of District Board
To appear in suits.
Counsel.
Secretary to keep full records.
Notice of meetings.

audited and paid as herein provided. He shall give ten days' previous notice of all regular and special meetings of the district by posting a written notice in five different conspicuous places therein, one of which shall be at or near the place of meeting of the district board. On or *Annual report.* before the twentieth day of September in each year, the secretary of each school district shall file with the Division Superintendent a report of the affairs of the district, which shall contain the following items, viz:

First—The number of persons, male and female each, *Persons in district.* in his district, between the ages of six and twenty-one years.

Second—The number of schools and the branches *Schools.* taught.

Third—The number of pupils, and the average attend- *Pupils.* ance of the same in the school.

Fourth—The number of teachers employed, and the average compensation paid per week, distinguishing males *Teachers.* from females.

Fifth—The length of school in days, and average cost *Time and cost of schools.* of tuition per week for each scholar.

Sixth—The aggregate amount paid teachers during the *Salary of teachers.* year, and the balance of teachers' fund in the treasury.

Seventh—The text books used, and the number of *Text books.* volumes in the district library, and value of apparatus belonging to the district.

Eighth—The number of school houses and their estima- *School houses.* ted value.

Ninth—The amount raised within the year by tax for the erection of school houses, the amount for teachers' *Tax.* fund and for other purposes of this act, stating separately the amount for each.

Tenth—The amount of public fund received from the parish treasury, and, if any, from other sources, stating *Public fund.* what, and how much from each, and such other informa- tion as he may deem useful. Should the Secretary fail to file his report, as above directed, he shall forfeit the sum of twenty-five dollars, and shall make good all losses *Penalty.* resulting from such failure; and suit shall be brought in

3

both cases by the district board on his official bond. The Treasurer shall hold all moneys belonging to the district and pay out the same on the order of the President, countersigned by the Secretary, and shall keep a correct account of all expenses and receipts in a book provided for the purpose. The money collected by district tax for school house purposes, and all contingent expenses, shall be called the "School House Fund," and that received for the support of teachers shall be called the "Teachers' Fund;" and the Treasurer shall keep with such fund a separate account, and shall pay no order which does not specify the fund on which it is drawn and the specific use to which it is applied. If he have not sufficient funds in his hands to pay in full the warrants drawn on the funds specified, he shall make partial payment thereon, paying as near as may be an equal proportion of each warrant. He shall receive all money apportioned to the district by the Superintendent of Public Education. He shall render a statement of the finances of the district from time to time, as may be required by law, and his books shall always be open for inspection.

SEC. 24. *Be it further enacted, etc.*, That it shall be the duty of the District Board of School Directors, between the first day of August and the fifteenth day of September of each year. to make and keep on record a list of the names of all heads of families in the district, and the number of children in each family between the ages of six and twenty-one years, distinguishing males from females, and to report the same to the Division Superintendent on or before the said fifteenth day of September, in each year. They shall further report the number of schools in their district, and the branches taught, the number of pupils and average attendance of the same in each school, the number of teachers and the compensation of each, the text books used, the number of school houses and the estimated value of each.

They shall have power to dismiss any pupils from the schools in their district for gross immorality, or for persistent violation of the regulations of the school, and to

Marginal notes: Treasurer. School house fund. Teachers' fund. Partial payments. Report. District Board to make list of names. Annual report. Dismission of pupils.

readmit them if they deem it proper so to do; and shall visit the schools in their district at least twice during each term of said school.

All contracts with teachers shall be in writing, specifying the length of time the school is to be taught, in weeks, the compensation per week, or per month of four weeks, and such other matters as may be agreed upon, and shall be signed by the director and teacher, and be approved by and filed with the president before any teacher shall be entitled to a warrant for services. — *Contracts with teachers.*

Sec. 25. *Be it further enacted, etc.*, That in each district there shall be taught one or more schools for instruction of youths between the ages of six and twenty-one years, for at least twelve weeks, of five school days each, in each year, unless the State Board of Education shall be satisfied that there is good and sufficient cause for failure so to do. — *Number and term of schools.*

Scholars residing in one district may attend school in another, in the same or adjoining parish, with the concurrence of the directors of both districts, and in such case, their proportion of the school money of the district to which they belong shall be paid to the treasurer of the district in which they attend school; and scholars may attend any school in the ward in which they reside, with the consent of the district board. — *Transfer of scholars.*

Sec. 26. *Be it further enacted, etc.*, That no parish or district school director shall receive any compensation for his services as director, or as an officer of the board. — *Compensation denied.*

Sec. 27. *Be it further enacted, etc.*, That each ward district shall hold regular meetings annually, on the first Saturday in May, at which all the qualified electors of the district may attend; *Provided*, That the first regular meeting of the qualified electors shall be held at such time as the Superintendent of Public Education may designate. Said meetings shall be presided over by the President of the District Board of School Directors, and the secretary of said board shall be the secretary of the meeting. — *Meetings of electors.*

The electors of a district, when legally assembled at a district school meeting, shall have power to levy such tax, not exceeding ten mills on the dollar in any one year, on the taxable property of the district, as the meeting shall deem sufficient, to purchase or lease a suitable site for a school house or school houses, and to build, rent or purchase a school house or school houses, and to keep in repair and furnish the same with the necessary fuel and appendages, and for compensation of teachers, and for procuring district libraries and apparatus for the schools, books and stationery for the board and district meetings, and defray all other contingent expenses of the district; *Provided,* That no tax shall be levied for building school houses, excepting at the regular meeting in May.

Whenever any tax has been voted at the regular meeting of the electors of a district, it shall be considered as by said vote levied upon the assessed value of all real and personal property in the district. The secretary of the meeting shall, within ten days thereafter, certify the same to the District Board of School Directors, who shall certify the number of mills of the tax thus levied to the collector of State taxes for the parish.

It shall thereupon be the duty of said collector to enter the same upon a separate assessment roll, which roll he shall, within ten days after he has been certified of the levy of the tax, submit to the District Board of School Directors, who shall examine, and, if correct, approve the same. The tax thus levied shall be collected in the same manner and by the same officer as State taxes, and shall be paid over quarterly, at such time as the District Board of School Directors may direct, to the treasurer of the district.

SEC. 28. *Be it further enacted, etc.,* That any person who shall be duly appointed as a parish or district school director, and shall refuse, neglect or fail to qualify according to law, and enter upon the performance of the duties of the office within ten days after official notification of his appointment, shall forfeit a sum not less than one hundred dollars, to be recovered by action before any

Power of electors to levy tax.

Property taxed.

Secretary to certify tax.

Assessment and collection of tax.

Penalty for failing to qualify.

court of competent jurisdiction. It shall be the duty of the district attorney to prosecute all such causes, and for each successful prosecution he shall receive as a fee twenty-five per cent. of the amount thus recovered. The State Board of Education shall report to each meeting of the General Assembly-the names of all persons so failing to serve, and the action had in each case by the district attorney; *Provided*, That no person disqualified by reason of ineligibility, or who shall be disabled by sickness from serving, shall be subject to the penalties of this section. All funds thus collected shall go to the school fund of the district or parish. *(District Attorney to prosecute)* *(State Board to report.)* *(Exceptions.)*

SEC. 29. *Be it further enacted, etc.*, That the State Board of Education shall have power to remove any parish or district school director for negligence, incompetency or violation of law, after a due hearing and fair trial. *(Removal of school directors.)*

SEC. 30. *Be it further enacted, etc.*, That the Superintendent of Public Education shall cause notice of the annual district meetings of the electors to be published in each parish, and, as far as possible, in each ward district, at least thirty days before such meetings. *(Notice of annual meetings.)*

SEC. 31. *Be it further enacted, etc.*, That the treasurer of the Board of Parish School Directors shall, immediately upon his appointment and qualification, receive from the parish treasurer all school funds that may be in the hands of the parish treasurer, and all records and accounts relating to any school funds. Any parish treasurer who shall fail on demand to turn over such funds and records to the treasurer of the Parish Board of School Directors, shall forfeit the sum of three hundred dollars, to be recovered by action before any court of competent jurisdiction, and shall, in addition, be liable upon his official bond with his sureties for any loss to the school funds or damage to the public interest that may be suffered thereby. From and after the passage of this act, the Auditor of Public Accounts shall issue no warrants upon any school fund to any parish treasurer. All claims upon such funds now held by parish treasurers shall be *(Parish treasurer to transfer school funds.)* *(Penalty for refusing to transfer funds.)* *(No warrants to be issued to parish treasurers.)*

examined by the State Board of Education, and referred by them to the next General Assembly.

SEC. 32. *Be it further enacted, etc.,* That all vacancies in any Board of Parish School Directors shall be filled by the State Board of Education; all vacancies in any District Board of School Directors shall be filled by the Parish Board of School Directors of the parish.

Filling vacancies.

QUALIFICATIONS AND DUTIES OF TEACHERS.

SEC. 33. *Be it further enacted, etc,* That no person shall be employed to teach a common school unless he shall have a certificate of qualification, signed by the Division Superintendent of the division in which the school is situated, or by the Superintendent of Public Education; and no certificate shall be valid more than one year from the date thereof; and any teacher who commences teaching without such certificate shall forfeit all claim to compensation for the time during which he teaches without such certificate.

Teachers' certificates.

Second—The teacher shall keep a correct register of the school, which shall exhibit the district, ward, parish and State in which the school is kept, the day of the week, the month and year, the name and age and attendance of each scholar, and the branches taught; the register to be after the form supplied by the Board of Education.

School register.

Third—When scholars reside in different districts, a register shall be kept for each district.

Fourth—The teacher shall, immediately after the close of his school, file in the office of the secretary of the board and transmit to the State Board of Education a certified copy of the register aforesaid.

Copy to be filed.

REVENUE.

SEC. 34. *Be it further enacted, etc.,* That for school purposes there shall be annually levied by the Auditor of Public Accounts, and collected by the collectors of State taxes, in the same manner as other State taxes are levied and collected, two mills upon the dollar upon all taxable property in the State. It shall be the duty of the Auditor of Public Accounts to notify the tax collectors of this

School revenue.

State tax.

assessment, and require the collection thereof. The tax collectors shall make separate monthly returns to the Auditor of Public Accounts (who shall transmit a copy thereof to the Superintendent of Public Education) of the collection of this tax, and pay the same into the State treasury.

SEC. 35. *Be it further enacted, etc.*, That the Superintendent of Public Education shall, quarterly, on the first Monday in March, June, September and December in each year, apportion the funds thus raised among the several ward, district, city or town school boards of the State, according to the number of children between the ages of six and twenty-one years, within the cities, towns or ward districts for which the respective boards have been appointed. The amounts so apportioned shall be paid by the State Treasurer to the treasurer of each such board upon the warrant of the president, countersigned by the secretary thereof. *Apportionment by State Superintendent.*

SEC. 36. *Be it further enacted, etc.*, That the State Board of Education may establish academies, normal schools and a teachers' institute, and provide for the government and control of the same. *Academies and normal schools.*

SEC. 37. *Be it further enacted, etc.*, That there shall be no public free schools within the State, not under the control of the boards of school directors herein provided for. The city of New Orleans, and other incorporated cities or towns, as well as all parochial authorities, are prohibited from organizing and maintaining separate public schools from those organized under this law, and controlled by the boards created hereby. It shall not be competent for any municipal or parochial authority to levy or collect any tax or impost to sustain schools not controlled by the boards acting under and by authority of this law. *Public schools not under State control interdicted.*

GENERAL PROVISIONS.

SEC. 38. *Be it further enacted, etc.*, That in the discharge of their duties in their several divisions, the Division Superintendents shall comply with such instructions of the Superintendent of Public Education as are *Division superintendents subject to instructions.*

not inconsistent with the provisions of this law, nor with the rules and regulations of the State Board of Education; and in case of failure to perform their duties as herein specified and provided, or for other improper conduct, the Superintendent of Public Education shall report the facts in the case to the Governor, who may remove such Division Superintendent and appoint a successor, as herein provided.

Governor may remove.

SEC. 39. *Be it further enacted, etc.*, That the offices of all School Directors, parish, city or district. and of all Division Superintendents, and of the members of the State Board of Education appointed or elected under any previous law, are hereby declared vacant, and upon the appointment of the officers provided for by this act, each and all of said officers shall, upon the demand of the officers appointed under this act, turn over all books, records and furniture of their offices to the officers thus appointed.

Offices vacated.

SEC. 40. *Be it further enacted, etc.*, That the fees of assessors for assessing any State school tax shall be one per cent. No fees shall be allowed any officer for assessing parish or district school taxes. The fees of collectors for collecting all school taxes shall be five per cent.

Fees of assessors and collectors.

SEC. 41. *Be it further enacted, etc.*, That the Treasurer of the Parish Board of School Directors in each parish is hereby required and authorized to examine the accounts of former parish treasurers with the school fund, and report all delinquencies and defaults in settlement and payment by any parish treasurer, to the State Board of Education, who shall report the same to the General Assembly. Upon the discovery of any such default or delinquency, the said treasurer of the Parish Board is authorized to prosecute suit in the name and for the use of said board against the delinquent or delinquents, and shall receive twenty-five per cent. of any and all amounts recovered by such prosecution. and paid to the parish school fund.

Treasurer of parish board to examine accounts, report and prosecute for default.

Sec. 42. *Be it further enacted, etc.*, That all officers appointed under this act shall take the oath of office prescribed by law. Oath prescribed

Sec. 43. *Be it further enacted, etc.*, That when any officer is superceded by appointment, he shall immediately deliver to his successor in office all books, papers and moneys belonging to his office, taking a receipt therefor. Every officer who shall refuse to do so, or who shall wilfully mutilate or destroy any such books or papers, shall be liable to a fine of not less than fifty nor more than five hundred dollars, at the discretion of the court. Books and papers to be surrendered. Penalty for withholding.

Sec. 44. *Be it further enacted, etc.*, That the Bible shall not be excluded from the public schools, but no pupil shall be required to read it contrary to the wishes of his parent or guardian. Bible in schools.

Sec. 45. *Be it further enacted, etc.*, That any officer, school, municipal, parish or State, or any teacher of any public school who shall refuse to receive into any school any child between the ages of six and twenty-one years, who shall be lawfully entitled to admission into the same, and shall comply with such rules and regulations as may be presented by the Board of School Directors and the State Board of Education, shall be deemed guilty of misdemeanor, and upon conviction thereof, shall be punished by a fine of not less than one hundred nor more than five hundred dollars, and by imprisonment in the parish jail for not less than one month nor more than six months, and all such causes shall have preference before other criminal cases upon the docket of the court before which it shall be brought; and such person so offending shall also be liable to an action for damages by the parent or guardian of the child so refused. Refusal to admit pupils. Penalty.

Sec. 46. *Be it further enacted, etc.*, That the police juries of the respective parishes shall be, and they are hereby authorized to levy a tax not exceeding two mills on the dollar, in any one year, on the taxable property of the parish; the same to be collected as other parish taxes, and under the same rules and regulations. The Parish school tax.

tax so collected shall be paid over by the tax collectors in the following manner, to wit: The amont of tax collected in any parish from property situated within the limits of a corporation, for which a separate board of school directors have been appointed, shall be paid to the treasurer of said board of school directors. The amount of tax collected from other property in the parish shall be paid to the treasurer of the Parish Board of School Directors. The funds so realized shall be apportioned by the Board of Parish School Directors among the several boards of district school directors in proportion to the number of persons between the ages of six and twenty-one years within their respective districts.

To whom to be paid.

Apportionment of parish school funds.

Sec. 47. *Be it further enacted, etc.,* That a school month shall consist of four weeks of five school days each. Any officer whose term of office is prescribed by this act shall continue in office until his successor is appointed and qualified.

School month.

Sec. 48. *Be it further enacted, etc.,* That all fines and penalties collected from a district officer by virtue of any of the provisions of this act, shall inure to the benefit of that particular district. Those collected from any member of the district board of school directors shall belong to the ward, and those collected from parish officers to the parish. In the two former cases suit shall be brought in the name of the district board of school directors; in the latter in the name of the parish and by the district attorney. The amount in each case shall be added to the fund next to be applied by the recipient for the use of common schools.

Fines and penalties.

Suits for penalties.

Sec. 49. *Be it further enacted, etc.,* That any person aggrieved by any decision or order of the district board of school directors, in matters of law or of fact, may, within thirty days after the rendition of such decision, or the making of such order, appeal therefrom to the superintendent of the proper district.

Aggrievances.

The basis of the proceeding shall be an affidavit, filed by the party aggrieved, with the Division Superintendent, within the time allowed for taking the appeal.

The affidavit shall set forth the errors complained of in a plain and concise manner.

Procedures in aggrievances.

The Division Superintendent shall, within five days after the filing such affidavit in his office, notify the secretary of the proper district, in writing, of the taking of such appeal. And the latter shall, within ten days after being thus notified, file in the office of the Division Superintendent a complete transcript of the record and proceedings relating to the decision complained of, which transcript shall be certified to be correct by the secretary.

Further proceedings.

After the filing of the transcript aforesaid in his office, he shall notify, in writing, all persons adversely interested, of the time and place where the matter of the appeal will be heard by him.

Filing of transcript.

At the time thus fixed for hearing, he shall hear testimony for either party, and for that purpose may administer oaths, if necessary, and he shall make such decision as may be just and equitable, which shall be final, unless appealed from, as hereinafter provided.

Hearing of the case.

An appeal may be taken from the decision of the Division Superintendent to the State Board of Education in the same manner as provided in this act for taking appeals from the decision of the District Board of School Directors to the Division Superintendent, as nearly as practicable, except that he shall give thirty days' notice of appeal to the Division Superintendent, and the like notice shall be given the adverse party. And the decision, when made, shall be final; *Provided*, That in cases which may arise when the State Board of Education are not in session, such appeal may be taken to the Superintendent of Public Education, who may decide the appeal, subject to the revision of the State Board of Education at its next meeting.

Appeals.

Nothing in this act shall be so construed as to authorize either the Division Superintendent or the State Board of Education to render a judgment for money; neither shall they be allowed any other compensation than is now allowed by law; *Provided*, That all necessary postage must first be paid by the party aggrieved.

Cases that involve money.

SEC. 50. *Be it further enacted, etc.*, That where lands shall be required for the erection of a school house, or for enlarging a school house lot, and the owner thereof shall refuse to sell the same for a reasonable compensa-

Lands taken for school purposes

tion, the District Board of School Directors shall have the power to select and possess such sites, embracing space sufficiently extensive to answer the purpose of school house and grounds. Should such landholder deem the sum assessed too small, he shall have the right to institute suit before any proper judicial tribunal for his claim, but the title shall pass from him to the school corporation.

Redress of land owner.

No person shall hold any office under the provisions of this act, unless he is a qualified voter of the State.

Voters only eligible to office.

A failure on the part of any district, parish or State officer to perform the duties imposed upon him in this act, and in the manner herein specified, is hereby declared a misdemeanor in office, upon conviction whereof such officer shall be punished by a fine not less than fifty and not exceeding one hundred dollars, and by imprisonment in the parish prison for a term of not less than thirty days, and not exceeding three months. All prosecutions for offenses against this section shall have precedence over all other cases before any justice of the peace, or parish or district court.

Failure to perform duties.

Nothing in this act shall be construed to apply to the State Seminary of Learning and Military Academy, it being the true intent and meaning of this act to leave that institution to be controlled by laws heretofore enacted concerning it.

State Seminary exempted from operation of this law.

The State Superintendent of Public Education shall make provision for model primary and grammar schools, under permanent and highly qualified teachers, in which the students of the normal school shall have opportunity to practice in the art of teaching. The salary of the teachers of the model and experimental schools shall be paid from the tuition fees derived from the pupils of said model schools, and those of the normal school who pay for their tuition; and any balance that may be required shall be paid by the State Board of Education out of the public school fund.

Model schools.

Salary of teachers.

SEC. 51. *Be it further enacted, etc.,* That in case any district board of school directors for any ward or any parish, city or town, or if the annual meeting of the qual.

Apportionment of school money withheld in certain cases.

ified electors of any such district shall refuse or fail to make suitable provision by purchase, lease or otherwise, for at least one school house in each district, to be used for school purposes at least four months in each year, and for the suitable furnishing and warming of the same, or to levy a sufficient tax for these purposes, no apportionment of any school fund made to such district by the Superintendent of Public Education, or by any other officers, under this act, shall be paid by any State, parish or city treasurer to the board of district school directors for such district.

It shall be the duty of the Superintendent of Public Education to notify the proper treasurers of any such delinquent districts, and such notification shall be the authority of such treasurer for the withholding of such payments. *Notification to treasurer.*

SEC. 52. *Be it further enacted, etc.*, That if, in any parish, before the month of December, in the years 1870 and 1871, the several District Boards of School Directors shall have failed to establish at least one school in a district, in one-half of the districts of the Parish, the Parish Board of School Directors are hereby empowered to make provisions for schools in the districts for which schools have not been provided, and for that purpose, after apportioning to the districts which may have established schools, their proportion of the parish school tax, said parish board may direct the expenditure of the remainder upon the schools established by said board. *Parish boards authorized to establish schools when district boards fail to do so.*

SEC. 53. *Be it further enacted, etc.*, That in the years eighteen hundred and seventy and eighteen hundred and seventy-one, whenever, in any parish, any or all of the school districts shall fail to levy a sufficient tax, and make suitable provision for at least one school house in the district, and for the payment of a teacher for at least two months, or when, in any or all of said school districts the District Directors shall have failed to qualify and enter upon the duties of their offices before the first day of December in each or either of said years, the State Superintendent may, upon the written report of the Parish Board of School Directors, setting forth the facts above named, direct the State Treasurer to withhold the apportionment *Provision for schools when district directors fail to qualify or to raise a sufficient tax.*

of the State school fund from said district or districts, and direct him to pay the same to the treasurer of the Parish Board of School Directors of such parish, and such parish board shall proceed to establish and conduct and maintain public schools in such district or districts, and may expend the funds from the State or parish school taxes of the district for that purpose.

PUBLIC SCHOOLS IN THE CITY OF NEW ORLEANS.

New Orleans city board of school directors.

SEC. 54. *Be it further enacted, etc.*, That in the city of New Orleans there shall be a Board of School Directors of eleven members, who shall hold their offices for two years, and until their successors are duly elected or appointed and qualified. At its first meeting after the passage of this act, the State Board of Education shall appoint six members of the said City Board of School Directors, and the Common Council of the city of New Orleans shall, as soon as possible after the passage of this act, elect five members thereof.

Powers and duties.

If the Common Council should fail or neglect, for three months after the appointments are made by the State Board of Education, to elect such members, the State Board of Education shall fill their places. Said Board shall have all the powers and perform all the duties in reference to the public schools of the city, and to the distribution of the school funds thereof, herein conferred upon the parish boards of school directors for other parishes. Said board shall hold its first meeting within thirty days after its appointment; shall choose a president and treasurer from its own members, and shall at once proceed to appoint, for each ward of the city of New Orleans, a ward board of school directors of five persons.

Ward school directors.

Secretary of city board.

SEC. 55. *Be it further enacted, etc.*, That the board of school directors for the city of New Orleans may elect a secretary, whose salary shall be eighteen hundred dollars ($1800) per annum, payable monthly, out of the public school fund, upon the warrant of the president of the board.

Each ward board a body corporate.

SEC. 56. *Be it further enacted, etc.*, That each ward board in the city of New Orleans, appointed under this act, shall be a body corporate by the name of the "Ward

School District of the city of New Orleans,' and in that name may hold property, sue and be sued, contract, and do other corporate acts.

SEC. 57. *Be it further enacted, etc.*, That each ward board of school directors in the city of New Orleans shall have the powers and duties, and be governed by the regulations herein prescribed for district boards of school directors in other parishes. Powers and duties.

SEC. 58. *Be it further enacted, etc.*, That each ward board of school directors for the city of New Orleans may, in their discretion, subdivide their ward into two or more sub-districts for school purposes, as may be deemed best for the public interest. Sub-districts.

The ward board of school directors for each ward shall convene an annual meeting of the qualified electors of each ward district on the first Saturday in May, of each year, which meeting shall have the powers and rights to levy taxes, and do other acts herein conferred upon the meeting of the qualified electors of ward districts in the parishes; *Provided,* Then whenever any ward board of school directors shall have subdivided the ward into sub-districts, the electors of each sub-district shall assemble on each first Saturday in May, in separate meetings, and such meeting for each such sub-districts shall have all the powers and rights to levy taxes, and do other acts herein conferred upon the annual meetings of the electors of ward districts in other parishes. Annual meeting of electors.

SEC. 59. *Be it further enacted, etc.*, That the ward boards of school directors for the city of New Orleans may allow children from one sub-district to attend the schools of another sub-district in the same ward or other wards, when they may deem it advisable. Transfer of scholars.

SEC. 60. *Be it further enacted, etc.*, That the treasurer of the board of school directors for the city of New Orleans, and the treasurer of each ward board of school directors, shall each give a bond in such sum and under such conditions for the faithful performance of his duty as the State Board of Education and Common Council may require. Treasurer's bond.

SEC. 61. *Be it further enacted, etc.*, That the control and direction of all public schools within said city, which Control vested in city board.

are supported from public school moneys, whether such moneys are derived from municipal or State taxation, is hereby vested in the board of school directors for the city of New Orleans, that shall be appointed under this act; and all laws or parts of laws by which the Common Council of New Orleans is empowered to elect a board of directors of the public schools, and by which any control over any of the schools named above, is given to said board of directors appointed or elected by the Common Council of New Orleans, and the special act of the General Assembly, approved March 14, 1855, entitled "An Act relative to public schools in the city of New Orleans," be and the same are hereby repealed.

Repeals previous enactments.

Sec. 62. *Be it further enacted, etc.,* That the sole and exclusive control and regulation of all public schools within the city of New Orleans, whether supported by municipal or State taxation, is hereby vested in the board of school directors for the city of New Orleans, and the other subordinate and local boards appointed in said city in accordance with the provisions of this act; and that the offices of all school directors in said city, appointed or elected, or assuming to act under authority of any law made prior to this act, are hereby terminated and made to cease; and all the powers hitherto conferred upon such school directors by virtue of any law or of any ordinance of said city, are hereby abolished and annulled.

Control of city schools.

Sec. 63. *Be it further enacted, etc.,* That the board of school directors appointed under and by virtue of this law shall at once apply to the person or persons now controlling the public schools in said city for possession of the books, furniture, apparatus and appendages in the possession of the said board of school directors for said city; that if said person or persons, or any person or persons shall usurp control of the public schools aforesaid, or shall fail or refuse to deliver said books, furniture, apparatus and appendages aforesaid, or shall assume or pretend to act as school directors for the city of New Orleans, in violation of law, he or they shall be deemed guilty of a misdemeanor, and shall, upon conviction of the fact, be fined each one thousand dollars, and imprisoned at the discretion of the court.

Application for books and papers.

Refusal to deliver school property.

Sec. 64. *Be it further enacted, etc.*, That if the validity of this law shall be questioned in any court, such suit shall have preference over all causes pending in such court.

Sec. 65. *Be it further enacted, etc.*, That this law shall not be construed so as to divest the city aforesaid of any property in the school houses or furniture in which public schools are held, but said property shall vest as now, in said municipal corporation, to be by it held in trust for public education under the laws of the State, and under the control and possession of the school boards appointed in accordance with this act.

Sec. 66. *Be it further enacted, etc.*, That the city of New Orleans be and is hereby prohibited from establishing or maintaining free public schools separate from those controlled by the officers appointed by this law.

Sec. 67. *Be it further enacted, etc.*, That no city or district school director, appointed in the city of New Orleans under this act, shall receive any compensation for his services. Any person so appointed and refusing or failing to qualify and enter upon the duties of his office within ten days after he shall be officially notified of his appointment, shall forfeit the sum of two hundred dollars ($200), to be recovered by the Superintendent of Public Education, before any court of competent jurisdiction, for the use of the school fund of the city.

Sec. 68. *Be it further enacted, etc.*, That all acts and parts of acts in conflict with this act are hereby repealed, and the charter of the city of New Orleans, and all laws or parts of laws, whether incorporated in the existing or any preceding charter of the city of New Orleans, or in any other statute of the State authorizing, requesting or empowering the Common Council of the city of New Orleans to establish and maintain public schools, or to elect school directors for the city of New Orleans, are wholly and expressly repealed.

SEC. 69. *Be it further enacted, etc.*, That this act shall take effect from and after its passage.

(Signed)   MORTIMER CARR,
   Speaker of the House of Representatives.

(Signed)   OSCAR J. DUNN,
  Lieutenant Governor and President of the Senate.

Approved March 16, 1870.

(Signed)   H. C. WARMOTH,
   Governor of the State of Louisiana.

A true copy:

  GEO. E. BOVEE,
   Secretary of State.

ALPHABETICAL INDEX.

	PAGE.	SECTION.

S

GENERAL ENACTMENTS

RELATING TO EDUCATION.

——•◦•——

DUTY OF SUPERINTENDENT IN REGARD TO SCHOOL LANDS.

From Section 29 of Act No. 321, of March 15, 1855.

SEC. 89. (29.) He shall, through the different district attorneys, inquire annually into the condition of the school sections, and institute such proceedings as may be necessary for their recovery when held illegally by individuals, or for the collection of claims originating in the sale of school lands which may be in arrears; and it shall be the duty of the District Attorney to prosecute the suits; *Provided,* The State Superintendent of Public Education shall be authorized to employ other counsel to prosecute these suits, on the refusal or neglect of the District Attorney to attend to the same. The money, when collected, shall be paid into the State treasury, and the interest thereof shall be placed to the credit of the district to which it belongs.

Inquire into condition of school sections.

FREE SCHOOL FUND.

From Sections 31 to 36 of Act No. 321 of March 15, 1855.

SEC. 90. (31.) The proceeds of all lands heretofore granted by the United States to this State for the use or support of schools, except the sixteenth section in the various townships of the States specially reserved by Congress for the use and benefit of the people therein: and of all lands which may hereafter be granted or bequeathed to the State, and not specially granted or bequeathed for any other purpose. which hereafter may

What constitutes free school fund.

be disposed of by the State, and the ten per cent. of the net proceeds of the sales of the public land which have accrued and are to accrue to this State under the act of Congress, entitlad "An Act to appropriate the proceeds of the public lands and to grant pre-emption rights:" approved September fourth, eighteen hundred and forty-one, and the proceeds of the estates of deceased persons, to which the State has or may become entitled by law, shall be held by the State as a loan, and shall be and remain a perpetual fund, to be called the Free School Fund, on which the State shall pay an annual interest of six per cent; which interest, together with the interest of the trust fund deposited with this State by the United States, under the act of Congress approved the twenty-third of June, eighteen hundred and thirty-six with the rents of all the unsold lands, except that of the sixteenth sections, shall be appropriated for the support of public schools in this State; and donations of all kinds which shall be made for the support of schools, and such other means as the Legislature may from time to time set apart for school purposes, shall form a part of the fund, and shall also be a loan on which the State shall pay an interest of six per cent. per annum.

DUTIES OF PARISH TREASURERS AS TO SCHOOL LANDS, ETC.

SEC. 91. (32.) It shall be the duty of the parish treasurers of the several parishes in this State, to have taken the sense of the inhabitants of the township to which may belong any lands heretofore reserved and appropriated by Congress for the use of schools, whether or not the same shall be sold, and the proceeds invested as authorized by an act of Congress approved February the fifteenth, eighteen hundred and forty-three, entitled an act to authorize the Legislatures of the States of Illinois, Arkansas, Louisiana and Tennessee to sell the lands heretofore appropriated for the use of schools in these States.

Polls shall be opened and held in each township, after advertisement for thirty days at three of the most public places in the township, and at the courthouse door, and

the sense of the legal voters therein shall be taken within
the usual hours, and in the usual manner of holding
elections, which elections shall be held and votes received
by a district director of public schools or a justice of the
peace; and if a majority of the legal voters be in favor of
selling the school land therein, the same may be sold, but
not otherwise. The result of all such elections shall be
transmitted to the Parish Treasurer, and by him to the
State Superintendent.

SEC. 92. (33.) Before making sale of the school lands
belonging to the State, it shall be the duty of the parish *Resurvey of lines.*
treasurer, or other persons whose duty it may become to
superintend the sales, to cause a resurvey of such lines
as from any cause may have become obliterated or uncer-
tain; and for this purpose he is authorized to employ the
parish surveyor, or, in his default, any competent surveyor, and the lines thus surveyed shall be marked in
such manner as to enable those interested to make a
thorough examination before sale; and all advertisements
made for the sale of such lands shall contain a full descrip-
tion thereof, according to the original survey and that
required by this section. The expenses of making the
survey shall be paid by the Auditor of Public Accounts,
out of the proceeds of the sale of the lands, on the
warrant of the parish treasurer.

SEC. 93. (34). (As amended and re-enacted by act
267, of 1858). If the majority of votes taken in a town- *Manner of con-ducting sales.*
ship shall give their assent to the sale of the lands afore-
said, the parish treasurer shall forthwith notify the Auditor of Public Accounts of the vote thus taken, and upon
his order the said lands shall be sold by the parish
treasurer at public auction, before the court house door,
or by the sheriff or an auctioneer, to be employed by the
treasurer at his expense, to the highest bidder, in quan-
tities of not less than forty acres nor more than one hundred and sixty, after having been previously appraised by
three sworn appraisers, selected by the parish treasurer
and recorder of the parish, after thirty days' advertisement; but in no case at a less sum than the appraised

value, payable on a credit of ten years, as follows, to wit: Ten per cent. in cash, and the balance in nine annual installments, the interest to be paid on the whole amount annually, at the rate of eight per cent. per annum. The notes shall be made payable to the Auditor of Public Accounts, secured by special mortgage on the land sold, and personal security, *in solido*, until final payment of principal and interest. In the event of the purchaser neglecting or refusing to pay any of these installments or interest at maturity, the mortgage shall be forthwith closed, and the parish treasurer is hereby authorized to advertise and sell the land as before provided for, and further authorized and required to execute all acts of sale on behalf of the State for any such lands sold, to receive the cash payments and notes given for the purchase, which shall be made payable to the State Treasurer, and to place the same in the office of the Auditor of Public Accounts for collection. All cash received, either for principal or interest from said sales, shall be transmitted by him to the State Treasurer, and any moneys thus received into the State treasury from sales aforesaid, shall bear interest at the rate of six per cent. per annum. and be credited to the township to which the same belongs, according to provisions of the act of Congress, The result of all sales made by the parish treasurer shall be forthwith notified by him to the State Superintendent. The parish treasurer shall be authorized to receive the whole amount bid for the lands, deducting the eight per cent. interest which the credits would bear.

DUTIES OF DISTRICT DIRECTORS AND PARISH TREASURERS AS TO UNSOLD SCHOOL LANDS.

Sec. 94. (35). Should a majority of the legal votes be
Lease of school lands against the sale of the lands, then it shall be the duty of the district directors where the same may be situated to secure them from injury and waste, and prevent illegal possession or aggression of any kind, and, in conjunction with the parish treasurer to lease the same, or any part thereof, for a term not exceeding four years, according to

the provisions of the second section of the act of Congress aforesaid, and to inform the State Superintendent thereof. Such lease shall only be made after due notice shall have been given by advertisement for at least thirty days, at two or more public places in the township, of the time and place when the land will be offered for lease, to the highest bidder. In all cases ample security shall be required not only for the punctual payment of the rent, but for the protection of the land from all and every kind of waste and injury.

DISPOSITION OF PROCEEDS OF LAND. ETC.

SEC. 95. (36). All moneys that have been or may be hereafter received into the State treasury, and the interest that has or may accrue thereon from the sale of the sixteenth section of school lands or the school land warrants belonging to the various townships in the State, shall be placed to the credit of the township; and should the people of any township desire to receive for the use of the schools therein the annual interest payable by the State on funds deposited to their credit, or the annual proceeds of the loans, the same shall be paid to the treasurer of the parish for the use of the townships or districts, otherwise the interest shall be an accumulating fund to their credit until so called for.

Disposition of proceeds of school lands.

FREE SCHOOL FUND IN STATE TREASURY.

From Sections 9 and 10 of Act No. 182 of March 19, 1857.

SEC. 96. (9). The interest due upon the capital (of the free school fund) and the interest due upon subsequent sales of the sixteenth sections shall be paid to the several boards of school directors of the districts in which the several sixteenth sections lie, on their own orders, approved by the treasurer of the parish, at any time within two years after the same shall be due. It shall be the duty of the Auditor of Public Accounts, at the end of every fiscal year, to notify the treasurers of all the parishes in the State of the amount of interest com-

Free school funds in treasury.

ing to the several townships within the limits of the parish, from the interest accrued during the year then terminated, and at the same time to furnish the State Treasurer and Superintendent of Public Schools with a tabular statement of the amount due to each township.

Sec. 97. (10). The rents of the sixteenth sections that may hereafter accrue shall not be paid into the State treasury, but shall be paid to the Parish Treasurer, and shall be subject to the order of the school directors of the districts in which the said sixteenth sections are located, and shall be by the said school directors appropriated to the support of their respective public schools.

Rents of sixteenth sections.

Act for Compensation to Parish Treasurer. No. 33, of March 12, 1859.

Sec. 98. The parish treasurers of the several parishes shall be entitled to retain, out of the proceeds of the sales of sixteenth sections effected by them, a per centage of two and one-half per centum on the amount of said sales, to be deducted from the cash payment, and the same shall be in full compensation of their services.

Compensation to parish treasurers.

Act (for Collection of Notes) No. 217, March 17, 1859.

Sec. 99. *First*—The Auditor of Public Accounts is hereby authorized and required to place the notes received from the sale of the sixteenth sections now due and those that hereafter fall due, in the hands of an attorney or attorneys for collection.

Second—The attorneys shall be allowed for collecting all such claims five per cent. and no more.

Collection of claims.

Act (for Relief of Purchasers) No. 83, of March 13, 1866.

Sec. 100. In all cases of the sale of the school lands known as sixteenth sections heretofore made, where the purchase money has not been paid, the purchaser or purchasers shall have the right to annul the sale upon application to the District Court of the parish where the land is situated; *Provided*, That the judgment of nullity shall

Annulment of sales by purchasers.

be obtained at the cost of the applicant and contradicto-
rily with the district attorney in conjunction with the
school directors in the district in which said land is situated, who shall be made a party defendant in such suit;
provided, also, that it shall appear upon the hearing that
the value of the land has not been impaired by any act
of the purchaser; *and provided further,* that nothing in
this act shall be so construed as to entitle the said purchaser to repayment of any part of the purchase money
already paid.

Act (Exempting Property of Public Schools from Seizure)
No. 151, *March* 14, 1855.

Sec. 101. Property dedicated to the use of and belonging to public schools, or employed by municipal cor-   Exempt from
porations for that purpose, shall be and is hereby ex-   seizure.
empted from seizure.

LAWS PROVIDING FOR THE FREE EDUCATION OF
TEACHERS.

Normal Department in High Schools—Organized in First
District of New Orleans, in 1858.

Sec. 102. Act to establish a Normal Department in the Public
High Schools in the city of New Orleans, No. 84, approved
March 15, 1858, as amended and re-enacted by Act No. 133
March 16, 1859.

First—The Directors of the public schools in the municipal districts of the city of New Orleans, are hereby   Normal school
authorized to establish in one or more of the Public High department.
Schools under their charge, a distinct class or division,
to be known as the Normal School Department, in which
those only shall be entered who desire to receive instruction in the art and science of teaching; said department
to contain not less than ten and not more than one hundred pupils, who shall remain therein not less than three
months nor longer than three years, and who shall previously, by written pledge, have declared their intention
of engaging in the occupation of teaching in the State of
Louisiana, for at least two years from the time when
diplomas shall have been awarded to them as graduates
of said department.

Second—For the support and encouragement of such
Normal School Department there shall be appropriated
out of the general fund of the State the sum of fifty dollars for each person receiving instruction therein, in
accordance with the conditions hereinbefore prescribed,
the said sum to be paid quarterly by the State Treasurer
upon the warrant of the Treasurer of New Orleans, drawn
on and approved by the Auditor of Public Accounts in
favor of the Directors in whose municipal districts such
departments shall have been organized; *Provided*, That
the session of said department shall be held on five days
of each week when not interrupted by national or State
holidays, or by annual vacations; and that the number of
scholars presented as the basis for appropriation shall be
in all cases the average attendance of scholars for the
previous quarter; *Provided, moreover*, That said directors
shall furnish satisfactory evidence of the actual establishment and successful operation of such department, and
that the total sum so appropriated shall not exceed five
thousand dollars per annum.

Third—The said Directors shall exercise exclusive control over such department and the teachers thereof, but
it shall be their duty to make a special annual report to
the Common Council of the city of New Orleans, and also
a similar report to the State Superintendent of Public
Education, during the first ten days of the month of January, showing in detail the condition of such department
under their charge, the number of pupils admitted and
left, the time of their continuance therein, and the actual
expense and the money received for the support of the
same.

Fourth—Whenever the number of graduated pupils
shall exceed the number of representative districts in
New Orleans, the Superintendent of Public Education
shall, upon application being made by the different parishes
distribute the excess among the parishes of the State in
such proportion as he may deem just and equitable.

Appropriation for support of.

Reports of.

Graduated pupils.

Act (Supplementary) constituting State Normal School, No. 155, *Approved March* 10, 1860.

SEC. 103.—The Normal School Department organized on the third day of April, 1858, and now in successful operation in the First District of the city of New Orleans, is hereby constituted and designated a State Normal School for the instruction and practical training of female teachers for the free public schools, and other educational institutions of Louisiana.

Said Normal School shall be open to applicants from every portion of the State who shall possess the qualifications of age, moral character, and mental culture prescribed by the Directors thereof, and who shall have declared their intention to adopt teaching as a profession to be exercised within the State of Louisiana for at least two years after they shall have received appropriate certificates or diplomas from said Directors. So soon as the Common Council of the city of New Orleans shall have provided the sum of ten thousand dollars to aid in the erection of a suitable building, the State will contribute a like sum, which is hereby conditionally appropriated to be paid in four equal installments within two years from the date of action of the Common Council, on the warrant of the Treasurer of New Orleans, approved by the Auditor of Public Accounts; and the title to said building and the site thereof, shall be exclusively in the State of Louisiana; *Provided,* That the Normal School therein accommodated shall be designated and organized in conformity to the provisions of the first and second sections of the act to which this is supplementary; and that the Directors thereof shall provide for the education of forty-eight pupils, to be selected by the Governor, and appointed annually; said pupils being entitled to remain in the school for two years, and to be educated free of charge for tuition, the State not paying the fifty dollars, as provided in the act to which this is supplementary, for any one of the forty-eight pupils so appointed.

The Directors of the State Normal School shall annually furnish the State Superintendent with an abstract

Normal schools in city of New Orleans for training of female teachers.

of the names, ages, residences, and qualifications of the
graduated pupils of said school, and from time to time,
with such other information as he may require.

NORMAL DEPARTMENT FOR EDUCATION OF MALE
TEACHERS IN STATE SEMINARY OF LEARNING, NEAR
ALEXANDRIA, LOUISIANA.

Sec] 104. Act (providing for Beneficiary Cadets) No. 131, March
28, 1867, amendatory of Section 10, of Act 98, of 1860, and of
Section 1, of Act 63, of 1866.

Each parish in the State shall have the right to delegate
to the State Seminary of Learning and Military Academy,
to remain four years, unless sooner graduated, a number
of beneficiary cadets corresponding with the number of
representatives to which such parish is entitled in the
House of Representatives, according to act approved
March 4, 1859, entitled an act to apportion the represen-
tation in the Senate and House in the General Assembly
of Louisiana, according to the second census, made in
1858, under the eighth and sixteenth articles of the constitution; that the Police Jury of each parish, and the Board
of School Directors of the city of New Orleans, respec-
tively, shall, at a regular meeting, to be held at least
twenty days prior to the first Monday of September, elect
such a number of beneficiary cadets as said parish or
city may be entitled to as aforesaid, of such age and
qualifications as may be prescribed by the Board of Supervisors of said Seminary, and cause the cadet or cadets
so selected to report in person at the Seminary on or before the said first Monday of September; *Provided*, That
such cadets as are now actually attending the Seminary
from any parish, or from the city of New Orleans, shall
be included in the number to which said parish or city is
entitled; *and provided further*, That in case of any vacancy in the delegation of any parish or of said city, an
election to fill the same shall be held at the first meeting
of said Jury or Board of Directors, after notice shall have
been given of said vacancy by the Superintendent of said
Seminary, and the cadets so elected shall be entitled to
admission into the Seminary at such time as the board of
supervisors shall prescribe; *and provided further*, That
the selection of said beneficiary cadets shall be made

Normal depart-
ment in state
seminary of
Learning.

from among those who have not themselves, or whose
parents have not the means of paying their expenses,
which facts shall appear by the certificate of the president of said jury or board of directors; and that said
beneficiaries whose education is thus provided for shall
be required at the close of their term at said institution
to pursue the occupation of teaching school within the
State for two years thereafter, and shall be required to
report such facts to the Superintendent of said institution; that the sum of four hundred dollars be and the
same is hereby annually appropriated for two years to
maintain and educate each of said beneficiary cadets,
payable quarterly, on the thirty-first day of March, the
thirtieth day of June, thirtieth day of September, and
the thirty-first day of December, to the treasurer of said
institution, upon the warrant of the Governor, and that
this act shall take effect from and after its passage.

SPECIAL PROVISIONS FOR THE FREE EDUCATION OF INDIGENT YOUNG MEN.

In Centenary College, Jackson, Louisiana.

SEC. 105. Acts Nos. 116 and 271, approved March 13 and 14, 1855.

It shall be the duty of the Faculty of Centenary College to have at all times in the institution, and to educate
gratuitously, ten indigent young men, to be designated
by the Governor of the State. *Centenary college.*

The college shall be subject to visitation by a committee
of the Legislature, and whenever the trustees shall fail
to perform any duty required of them by the law, or
whenever they shall establish a chair of theology or make
sectarian dogmas any part of their course of study, then,
and in either of the above cases, the bond heretofore
given by them to the State shall be due, and the Treasurer
shall proceed to collect it, with legal interest from the
time of such forfeiture.

The Board of Trustees of said college shall, after the
year eighteen hundred and fifty-five, receive from each
Congressional district three indigent students, free from
charge for tuition, in addition to the number of indigent
students now required by law to be educated in said *Indigent students.*

college; said indigent students to be nominated by the Governor of the State; *Provided*, That no more than twelve students shall at any one time be domiciliated within the walls of said college under the provisions of this section. Each pupil so received shall be entitled to four years tuition, and no indigent student to be admitted in said college before he has arrived at his thirteenth year.

In University of Louisiana, New Orleans.

SEC. 106. Act (relative to University) No. 320. March 15, 1855.

University of Louisiana.

The faculties of the University may admit, free of charge, such number of indigent young men of the State, of good abilities and correct moral deportment, as they may deem expedient.

FREE PASSAGE OF CHILDREN OVER PUBLIC FERRIES AND ROADS.

Act No. 162, of October 17, 1868.

Free Passage of children over public ferries and roads.

SEC. 107. (1). The free right of passage or conveyance over all the public ferries, bridges and roads (except the ferries on the Mississippi river), which are rented out by the State or parish, or over which the State or parish exercise any control, or for which license is paid or toll exacted, is hereby granted to all children on foot attending free public schools, and no tolls or fees shall be demanded or exacted from said children by the keepers or attendants of said ferries, bridges or roads in their passage to or from school, between the hours of seven o'clock A. M. and nine o'clock A. M., and four o'clock P. M. and six o'clock P. M.; *Provided*, That on Sundays and school holidays, no scholar shall have the right to cross such ferries, bridges or roads on terms different from those of any ordinary passenger.

Lessees of public ferries.

(2). This act shall have effect from and after the establishment of free public schools throughout the State, and it shall not apply to any lessee of a public ferry whose contract or lease was made previous to the date of this act.

EDUCATIONAL BUILDINGS EXEMPT FROM TAXATION.

From Section 2 of Act No. 114, approved March 9, 1869.

Sec. 108. (2). The following property shall be exempt from taxation: *   *   *   *   * Educational buildings exempt from taxation.
*   *   * Colleges, school houses, and other buildings for the purpose of education, and their furniture, apparatus and equipments, and the lots thereto appurtenant and used therewith, so long as actually used for that purpose only.   *   *   *   *   *   *

8

RULES AND REGULATIONS

FOR THE

GOVERNMENT OF SCHOOLS

AND

Subordinate Boards of School Directors,

BY THE

STATE BOARD OF EDUCATION,

STATE OF LOUISIANA.

RULES AND REGULATIONS.

CHAPTER I.—GRADES—BRANCHES OF STUDY.

RULE 1.—The different grades of schools in the State of Louisiana shall be designated as Primary, Grammar, High and Normal Schools.

RULE 2.—In the Primary Schools there shall be taught the rudiments of reading, writing, spelling and arithmetic. In the Grammar Schools there shall be taught reading, writing, arithmetic, English grammar, geography and history of the United States; and, where practicable, vocal music and drawing.

RULE 3.—The Primary and Grammar Schools shall contain four grades of departments, known as First and Second Primary, and First and Second Grammar departments; but in sparsely settled districts of country, the Primary and Grammar Schools may be united at the discretion of the local boards.

RULE 4.—The High Schools shall be for the education of all children who are competent to pursue the branches taught therein.

CHAPTER II.—TERMS AND SCHOOL SESSIONS.

RULE 5.—The scholastic year shall commence on the first Monday in September; and in every school district there shall be kept, for at least twenty-four weeks in each year, at such times as the local board may deem most convenient, a sufficient number of schools for the instruction of all the children who may legally attend public schools therein.

RULE 6.—There shall be daily sessions in all the schools, Saturdays, Sundays and holidays excepted. These sessions shall be regulated as to their duration and intermissions by the District Boards, but it is hereby recommended that the sessions, exclusive of recess, shall not exceed five hours each day.

CHAPTER III.—EXAMINATIONS.

Rule 7.—A public examination of all the schools shall take place at least once in each year; besides which all the classes in the High and Normal Schools shall be examined, in writing, in each branch of study when it is completed.

CHAPTER IV.—VACATIONS AND HOLIDAYS.

Rule 8.—The schools shall be closed from the twenty-fifth of December to the first of January, inclusive; on all thanksgiving or fast days authorized by the State or General Government, and on all Saturdays throughout the year, and on such other days as may be directed by the District Boards.

CHAPTER V.—TEACHERS.

Rule 9.—Teachers are required to be at their respective rooms at least ten minutes before the time for opening each session, and shall, in a daily register to be kept by the principal, record their names and hour and minute of their arrival, and any teacher failing to comply with this rule shall be reported by the principal as tardy.

Rule 10.—They shall open school punctually at the appointed time, devote themselves during school hours exclusively to the instruction of their pupils, maintain good order, and strictly adhere to the course of study and the use of the text books.

Rule 11.—It shall be their duty to practice such discipline in their school as would be exercised by a kind and judicious parent in his family, always firm and vigilant, but prudent. They shall endeavor, on all proper occasions, to impress upon the minds of their pupils the principles of morality and virtue, a sacred regard for truth, love to God, love to man, sobriety, industry and frugality. But no teacher shall exercise any sectarian or political influence in the schools. The free schools of this State are open to all without regard to religious belief, and, while recognizing the Bible as the source of all true religion, and while its public reading in the schools is earnestly recommended, yet should objection be made thereto by any of the parents or guardians of children attending, such reading shall be omitted.

Rule 12.—They shall see that the pupils under their charge distinctly understand and faithfully observe all the rules relating to pupils.

Rule 13.—They shall attend carefully to the ventilation and temperature of their school rooms.

Rule 14.—Any teacher who may be absent from school on account of sickness, or other necessity, must cause immediate notice of such absence to be given to the Directors. Teachers absent from their places, without satisfactory cause, for three successive days, may be considered as having resigned.

Rule 15.—No teacher shall resign without giving two weeks' written notice to the President of the Board or Sub-Director, in default of which, all compensation due for one half-month may be forfeited.

Rule 16.—The salary of teachers shall be deducted *pro rata* for absence, except in cases of duly attested illness.

Rule 17.—No teacher shall be employed in the public schools who does not hold a certificate of qualification from the State or Division Superintendent.

Rule 18.—Teachers shall not hold any position of higher grade than the one corresponding to their certificates.

CHAPTER VI.—PRINCIPAL TEACHERS.

Rule 19.—The principal teachers shall keep a register, in which they shall record the name, age, birth place, residence and date of admission of each pupil for the first time entered in the public schools, and also the name and occupation of the parent or guardian.

Rule 20.—They shall also make a daily record of the pupils admitted, present, absent or tardy (provided that no pupil shall be considered as enrolled after five consecutive days' absence), and at the close of each term they shall file the same in the office of the Secretary of the District Board, and at the close of the school year shall forward two certified copies of said records to the Division Superintendent, one of which shall be forwarded to the State Board.

Rule 21.—The principal shall have a general supervision of the grounds, buildings and appurtenances of the school, and shall be held responsible for any want of neatness or cleanliness on the

9

premises; whenever any repairs are needed he shall give notice thereof to the President of the District Board.

RULE 22.—Each principal shall examine the classes of the assistants as often as practicable, without neglecting the pupils under his immediate charge.

RULE 23.—No distinction shall be made by any Board of School Directors by which female teachers shall receive less pay than is allowed to males, when the services rendered are equal.

CHAPTER VII.—CONCERNING DISCIPLINE.

RULE 24.—All teachers are required to maintain strict order and discipline in their schools. Any neglect of this requirement will be considered good cause for dismissal. In maintaining order teachers are hereby authorized to employ any proper means which may be necessary to secure a compliance with their commands to the pupils, and in the use of which they will receive the full countenance and support of the District Board.

RULE 25.—All teachers will be held to a strict accountability as to the manner in which they shall use the authority herein delegated, and upon complaint of severity of punishment, each case shall be adjudged upon its own merits, the teacher being subject to dismissal if the Board decide it to be demanded by the circumstances.

RULE 26.—Those teachers who are most successful in maintaining the order and discipline of their pupils without the use of corporal punishment, other qualifications being sufficient, shall be awarded by the Board a higher degree of appreciation, and receive the preference over all others in promotions and appointments.

RULE 27.—Principals shall be permitted, without interference on the part of any member of the Board, except on the recommendation of the Superintendent, to arrange the details for the internal government of their schools according to their own method, provided such method is not inconsistent with the general regulations of the schools.

RULE 28.—The principals shall be required, within one week after the commencement of each term, to have the programme of their daily exercises posted in the school room in a conspicuous place, and shall transmit a copy of the same to the President of the District Board, and one to the Division Superintendent.

CHAPTER VIII.—PUPILS—ADMISSION, ATTENDANCE AND ABSENCE.

RULE 29.—Children applying for admission into the public schools are required to furnish all the necessary text books and stationery used in their classes.

RULE 30.—No one having been a pupil in one school shall be admitted into another during the same scholastic year, without presenting to the principal a certificate of honorable discharge from the former school.

RULE 31.—No pupil shall be allowed to depart from school before the usual time, unless sick, or on account of some other pressing emergency, of which the teacher shall be the judge.

CHAPTER IX.—DEPORTMENT OF PUPILS.

RULE 32.—The pupils must, on all occasions, be obedient to their teachers and polite in their intercourse with each other. They must be diligent in study, prompt in recitation, and observe propriety of deportment during the recesses, and in coming to and going from school.

RULE 33.—Cleanliness in person and clothing is required of every pupil, and repeated neglect or refusal to comply with this rule shall be sufficient cause of suspension from school.

RULE 34.—Any pupil who shall willfully destroy or injure any property of the public schools shall be required to pay the amount lost thereby, and on failure to do so may be suspended from school.

RULE 35.—Any pupil guilty of disobedience to a teacher, or of gross misconduct, may be suspended by the principal, written notice of which, stating the cause, shall be immediately given to the parent or guardian, and to the District Board.

RULE 36.—Any pupil suspended from school by virtue of any of the above rules, can be restored only on such conditions as the Board of Directors shall determine.

CHAPTER X.—SCHOOL DIRECTORS.

RULE 37.—The Secretaries of the District Boards of School Directors shall, in addition to the regular reports required of them by law, to their respective Division Superintendents, make, in connection therewith, full and complete reports of all school lands in their districts, the amount and condition of the same, and any changes that may occur therein by sale, rent, or otherwise, and shall make it their especial care to see that such lands are not trespassed upon, or in any way laid to waste, and will make such other reports as the State or the Division Superintendents may at any time direct.

RULE 38.—If, in any ward of any parish, an organization cannot be effected for school purposes, through lack of suitable persons to be appointed as school directors or otherwise, such ward shall be merged into the ward next most contiguous, forming one school district therewith, the Superintendent of the Division designating with what contiguous ward it shall be merged, and the Board of School Directors of the ward to which such unorganized district is joined, shall assume charge of the same, until such time as said ward can be satisfactorily organized.

RULE 39.—The constitution of the State of Louisiana declares that "all children of this State, between the ages of six and twenty-one years, shall be admitted to the public schools or other institutions of learning sustained or established by the State, in common, without distinction of race, color or previous condition." In accordance with this provision every District Board and teacher shall admit any child entitled to admission to any of the public schools established in any city, parish, ward or town under authority of law.

OFFICE STATE BOARD OF EDUCATION,
New Orleans, April 8, 1870.

The foregoing rules and regulations were this day adopted by a unanimous vote of the Board.

T. W. CONWAY,
President of Board,

WILLIAM ROLLINSON,
    Secretary of Board,

APPENDIX.

———•••———

CURRENT SCHOOL FUND.

This fund was first created by act No. 200, approved March 19, 1857, and now consists:

1. Of the two mill tax, as provided in the fifty-seventh section of the foregoing compilation, and is estimated at a maximum of about $460,000.
2. Of ninety per cent. of the poll tax as provided in the fourth (5th) section of act No. 114, approved March 9, 1869, estimated at $36,000.
3. Of amount accruing from the license of the Louisiana State Lottery Company, article 5, section 1, act No. 25, of 1868, $40,000.

Section 2 of the first act above mentioned requires that the current school fund shall be used for the support of public schools, and that the surplus of receipts over expenditures for any one year, shall be appropriated to the support of such schools during the ensuing year.

The appropriation out of this fund, for 1869, is $250,000.

Sections 57 and 58, of the foregoing compilation, define the Auditor's duties in relation to said fund; sections 21, 29, 55 and 58, those of the Treasurer.

FREE SCHOOL ACCUMULATING FUND.

The Free School Accumulating Fund was created by act No. 265, approved March 14, 1855, and is derived from—

1. The interest on the vested proceeds of school lands (1211 bonds, representing $1,193,500) annually, $71,610.
2. The interest on bonds belonging to the "Free School Fund," remaining due after payment to townships.
3. The receipts from sales of sixteenth sections.
4. The ten per cent. tax on estates descending to foreign heirs, and other funds received in trust for free school purposes. (See section 89 of Compilation).

The Auditor and Treasurer are required to invest such funds, with the Governor's sanction, in stocks, bonds of the State, or bonds of the consolidated city of New Orleans, bearing six per cent. interest, and hold said investment sacred for the accumulation of a fund sufficient to produce, by the dividends derived from it, an amount equal to that required annually for the support of free public schools.

Section 2, of act No. 200, of 1857, repeals other provisions of this act, and those of act No. 181, of 1855. As to such investment and the interest thereon, see act No. 182, of March 19, 1857, ("in relation to certain debts of the State"); sections 1, 2 and 3, in lieu of section 7, repealed; see section 2, of act No. 48, of March 6, 1858; and sections 8, 9, 10, 11, 12 and 13, of act No. 182, of 1857; and finally, act No. 26, of March 12, 1859.

Section 13 and act No. 26 provide that the receipts constituting the "Free School Accumulating Fund," shall not be mingled with any other moneys in the Treasury, and that the Auditor and Treasurer shall annually report to the Governor the amount belonging to said fund, and invest it in any of the bonds receivable by the State, as securities for the circulation of the banks established under the Free Banking Law.

Section 12 makes the Secretary of State and the State Treasurer joint custodians of the Free School Bonds, and the Auditor the collector of the interest coupons thereto attached.

II—STATE SEMINARY OF LEARNING AND MILITARY ACADEMY.

ESTABLISHED NEAR ALEXANDRIA, LA.

Act for Organization and Government, No. 228, of March 15, 1858—as subsequently amended, and now in force.

Section 1. (As re-enacted by section 1, act No. 98, approved March 7, 1860). The "State Seminary of Learning," established near the town of Alexandria, in the parish of Rapides, shall be hereafter designated as "The Louisiana State Seminary of Learning and Military Academy," and shall be under the direction and control of fourteen supervisors, who shall be a body corporate, under the style and title of the "Board of Supervisors of the Louisiana State Seminary of Learning and Military Academy," with the right, as such, to use a common seal, and who shall be capable in law to receive all donations, subscriptions and bequests in trust for said Seminary and Academy, and to recover all debts which may become the property of said Seminary and Academy, and to sue and be sued in courts of justice; and in general to do all acts for the benefit of the Seminary and Academy which are incident to bodies corporate.

SEC. 2. (As re-enacted by act No. 14, approved February 14, 1870). The Governor of the State shall be *ex officio* President of the Board of Supervisors, and the Chief Justice of the Supreme Court, the Superintendent of Public Education, and the State Engineer shall be *ex officio* members of said Board. The remaining ten members thereof shall be appointed by the Governor, by and with the advice and consent of the Senate, for four years; and they shall continue to exercise the duties of their office until their successors are qualified, and shall be removed by the same power and in the same manner as provided for in their appointment. The Governor shall select ten members, as follows: three from the parish of Rapides, two from the parish of Orleans, and five from the remaining parishes; *Provided*, That not more than one member shall be selected from any one of the said remaining parishes.

Said Board shall elect one of the members from Rapides as Vice-President, to serve in the place and absence of the Governor; the three members from the parish of Rapides shall constitute an Executive Committee, to be convened by the President or Vice President, for the transaction of such urgent business and important business as, in the opinion of the President or Vice President, cannot be delayed till a meeting of the Board of Supervisors can be convened; and the proceedings of the Executive Committee shall be submitted to the Board of Supervisors for approval or disapproval at the first meeting of the said Board subsequent to the meeting of the Executive Committee. The Board of Supervisors and the Executive Committee shall hold their meetings at any point designated by the President or Vice President of the Board; *Provided*, That one meeting shall be held annually at the State Seminary and Military Academy at the time of the commencement exercises of said Academy.

SEC. 3. (Act No. 98, March 7, 1860, as modified by foregoing second section, 1867). The Board of Supervisors shall have stated meetings at such times as the President or Vice President of said Board shall deem necessary to convene them, a majority of the whole Board constituting a quorum for the transaction of business, but any Supervisor who shall fail to attend two consecutive meetings shall be deemed and considered as refusing to act as such, and upon such failure to attend being notified to the Governor, he shall proceed to the appointment of his successor, in the same manner as hereinbefore prescribed; *Provided*, That if such failure be occasioned by sickness or temporary absence from the State, the provisions of this section shall not apply thereto; *Provided, however*, That any four members of the board, together with the President or Vice President, shall be a sufficient quorum for the transaction of business.

SEC. 4. (Act No. 98, March 7, 1860, amending section 5 of act of 1858). The Board of Supervisors shall have power to engage a superintendent and other professors, and all other officers necessary for conducting the literary, financial and civil concerns and interests of the said Seminary and Academy, and to remove and displace the same at pleasure; to fix and regulate the salaries of the professors, and all other officers, tuition fees, and all other charges; to establish rules for the good government and discipline of the students; to prescribe the duties of all officers, servants, and others; to confer diplomas, upon the recommendation of the superintendent and faculty, on students for proficiency in any branch of science or department of learning; and in general to make all rules and regulations which may be deemed necessary for the proper government of the said Seminary and Academy, and for promoting the objects for which it was founded; but nothing in this act shall be construed as obligating the State to pay any debts contracted by the Board of Supervisors, in case they should at any time exceed the appropriations made for the support of said Seminary and Academy.

SEC. 5. (6th of act No. 228, March 15, 1868). The Board of Supervisors shall, at their first meeting, elect a secretary, who shall record, attest, and preserve their proceedings, and a treasurer, who shall give bond for the faithful performance of his duties, and in such sum as shall be determined by the Board.

NOTE.— Sections 7, 8, 9 and 10 of act of 1858, refer to the original board of trustees, and the first board of supervisors, exclusively, except as to the following provisions, which are still in force :

SEC. 6. It shall be the duty of the Board of Supervisors, immediately after their organization, to prescribe the course of studies to be pursued at the Seminary, and the number of professors, and to draw up a project of the system of instruction so adopted.

SEC. 7. The Board of Supervisors shall be charged with the preservation and repair of the buildings of the Seminary, and the care of the grounds and appurtenances.

NOTE.—Sections 3, 11, 12 and 13 of the act of 1858 have been repealed by acts of 1860, '66 and '67.

SEC. 8. (6th of act No. 98, of March 15, 1860). In the course of study pursued at the said Seminary and Academy. the Board of Supervisors shall cause instructions to be given in the military branches of science; the students shall be called cadets, and shall compose a military corps, under the command of the superintendent and such other professors as may be assigned to that branch of instruction. They shall constitute a guard to all public property, arms, or munitions now there, or which may hereafter be assembled there; and the superintendent shall receipt for all such property, arms, or munitions, and shall obey all orders relative to their preservation or delivery, as he may receive from the Governor of the State.

SEC. 9. (7). The Governor of the State shall cause to be issued to the superintendent a commission as colonel, and to such other professors as may be assigned to command, commissions as majors, captains, or lieutenants, according to the strength of the command; *Provided,* That such commissions shall not entitle the holders to any rank in the militia of the State, or to any claim whatever to compensation other than what is attached to their positions as professors.

NOTE.—See, in this connection, act No. 202, of March 14, 1860, "providing for the establishment of a 'central State arsenal,' in connection with the Seminary," etc., and act No. 15, of February 19, 1867, "requesting the Secretary of War to revoke his order forbidding the usual military exercises at the Seminary, and to permit their resumption, as has been done at similar institutions in other States."

SEC. 10. (8th of act No. 98, of 1860). The reasonable expenses of the Supervisors, in going to and attending the meetings of the Board, shall be paid by the State; and it shall be the duty of the Board of Supervisors to set forth in their annual report the amount of such expenses.

NOTE.—The remainder of this section has been repealed.

SEC. 11. (10th of act No. 98, of 1860). *Proviso:* The beneficiary cadets (in the State Seminary) shall be placed on a footing of perfect equality with the paying cadets in said institution; and it shall

10

be the duty of said Board of Supervisors to report to the Legislature the exact costs incurred in supporting a cadet.

Note.—The tenth section of the act 98, of 1860, in so far as it provided for beneficiary cadets, was amended by the first section of act No. 63, approved March 7, 1866, and this first section was re-amended and re-enacted by act No. 131, approved March 28, 1867, which said act appears hereinbefore as section 103 of the compilation.

Sec. 12. (Section 2, of act No. 63, of March 7, 1866). The State Librarian is directed and required to turn over to the superintendent of said institution copies of any books of which there may be duplicates in the library of the State, for the use of the "Louisiana State Seminary and Military Academy," taking therefor the receipt of said superintendent, which shall be filed in the office of the State Librarian as his vouchers for said books, when called upon to produce or turn over the same.

Sec. 13. (Section 2, of act No. 162, of March 28, 1867). No gambling house or drinking saloon, or store for the barter or sale of any kind of merchandise whatever, shall be established within two miles of said institution.

Sec. 14. (Of act No. 228, approved March 18, 1858). The Board of Supervisors shall at all times conform to such laws as the Legislature may, from time to time, enact for their government, and the said Seminary shall in all things and at all times be subject to the control of the Legislature; and the said Board of Supervisors shall make an annual report to the Legislature during the first week of the session, embracing a full account of the disbursements, and a general statement of the condition of said Seminary.

SEMINARY FUND.

(See Article 136, of Constitution of 1845; Article 138 of that of 1852, and Article 145, of that of 1864.)

This fund is vested in the same manner as the "Free School Accumulating Fund," under act No. 182, of March 19, 1857, already referred to. It consists of one hundred and thirty-eight bonds, representing $138,000, bearing six per cent. interest per annum. (See Auditor's Report of January 1, 1869.)

The appropriations for the re-organization and support of the Seminary, in 1866, 1867 and 1869, have been as follows:

Act No. 63, of March 7, 1866.

Interest on fund for 1863, 1864 and 1865	$25,800
For repairs and refitting of building, outhouses, etc.	5,000
For renewal of library, apparatus, etc., destroyed or lost during war	5,000
For maintenance of 52 beneficiary cadets, at $300	15,600
For salary of secretary, traveling expenses of supervisors, stationery and incidentals	1,000
Total for 1866	$52,400

Act No. 131, of March 28, 1867.

For maintenance of 98 beneficiary cadets, at $400	$39,200

Act No. 153, of March 28, 1867.

For defraying expenses of supervisors	1,000

Act No. 162, of March 28, 1867.

For additional repairs to buildings and improvement of grounds	5,000
For enlarging the library and philosophical apparatus	5,000

Act No. 119, of March 25, 1867.

Interest on fund for 1862 and 1866	16,380
Total for 1867	$66,580

Act No. 73, of March 6, 1869.

For the erection of three professors' houses	$15,000
For repairs to buildings as now erected	5,000
For the erection of additional outhouses	5,000
For purchase of additional philosophical apparatus and library books	5,000
For traveling expenses of board of supervisors for year 1869	1,000

Act No. 139, of May 25, 1869.

Interest on fund for 1869	8,220
For expenses of 98 cadets one year, at $40 per month	39,200
Total for 1869	$78,420

Payable to treasurer of Seminary on warrant of the Governor.

III.—UNIVERSITY OF LOUISIANA.

IN NEW ORLEANS.

This University, per act No. 81, of March 3, 1860, is under the control and supervision of eleven administrators, of which body the Governor, Chief Justice of the State and the Mayor of New Orleans are *ex officio* members, the remaining eight being appointed every four years by the Governor, by and with the advice and consent of the Senate. The administrators receive no compensation for their services.

The powers and duties of administrators are defined in section 2 *et seq.* of act No. 320, approved March 15, 1855. Of the four departments or faculties, of which the University should be composed, according to said act, and the 143d Article of the constitution of 1864, but two have been organized, viz : those of Law and Medicine. (See Art. 142, of constitution 1868).

The appropriations in 1866 and 1867 " for the relief of the University," have been as follows :

Act No. 130, March 22, 1866.

For repairs of buildings and to maintain the University....$25,000

Act No. 182, of March 28, 1867.

For fitting up library, lecture and professors' rooms, and completing repairs 3,000

Total..$28,000

IV.—INSTITUTIONS OF LEARNING GENERALLY.

Act No. 267, approved March 14, 1855.

SECTION 1. The president and trustees of any institution of learning established in the State of Louisiana, which is or may be hereafter incorporated as a body politic, in conformity with the constitution and laws of the State, who may wish so to do, can deposit in the treasury of the State of Louisiana, all sums of money intended solely for the uses and purposes of such institutions of learning; and all sums so deposited shall be invested in the bonds or obligations of the State of Louisiana or of the United States, and the interest accruing thereon, as realized, shall be paid over to such corporation, or again invested as they may desire.

SEC. 2. Should any endowment be made, either by donations *inter vivos* or *mortis causa*, to establish a professorship, in any institution of learning in the State duly incorporated, on the principal being deposited in the State Treasury, the same shall be invested, and the interest as realized shall be paid over as stipulated in the preceding section; and it shall be the duty of the Auditor of Public Accounts and the State Treasurer to make the investments to the greatest advantage and interest of said institution.

MISCELLANEOUS APPROPRIATIONS, ETC., FOR THE BENEFIT OF EDUCATION.

Act No. 156, of March 22, 1866.

For purchase of 2666 copies of Spencers's English Grammar for gratuitous distribution throughout the State (from Current School Fund)............................... $2,000

Act No. 184, of March 28, 1867.

For repairs to Poydras College, parish of Pointe Coupée, (from Current School Fund)............................... $2,500

Act No. 154, of March 28, 1867.

Lands belonging to the State laboratory at Mount Lebanon, Bienville parish, donated to trustees for the use and benefit of Mount Lebanon Female College.....................

Act No. 163, of October 19, 1868.

For Third District Indigent Orphan School, Greatmen street, New Orleans.. $2,500

V.— CONSTITUTION OF 1868, TITLE VII.

PUBLIC EDUCATION.

ARTICLE 135. The General Assembly shall establish at least one free public school in every parish throughout the State, and shall provide for its support by taxation or otherwise. All children of this State, between the ages of six (6) and twenty-one (21) years, shall be admitted to the public schools or other institutions of learning sustained or established by the State, in common, without distinction of race, color or previous condition. There shall be no separate schools or institutions of learning established exclusively for any race by the State of Louisiana.

ART. 136. No municipal corporation shall make any rules or regulations contrary to the spirit and intention of article one hundred and thirty-five (135).

ART. 137. There shall be elected by the qualified electors of this State a Superintendent of Public Education, who shall hold his office for four years. His duties shall be prescribed by law, and he shall have the supervision and the general control of all public schools throughout the State. He shall receive a salary of five thousand dollars per annum, payable quarterly, on his own warrant.

ART. 138. The general exercises in the public schools shall be conducted in the English language.

ART. 139. The proceeds of all lands heretofore granted by the United States, for the use and support of public schools, and of all lands or other property which may hereafter be bequeathed for that purpose, and of all lands which may be granted or bequeathed to the State and not granted or bequeathed expressly for any other purpose, which may hereafter be disposed of by the State, and the proceeds of all estates of deceased persons to which the State may be entitled by law, shall be held by the State as a loan, and shall be and remain a perpetual fund, on which the State shall pay an annual interest of six per cent., which interest, with the interest of the trust fund deposited with this State by the United States, under the act of Congress, approved June 23, 1836, and the rent of the unsold lands, shall be appropriated to the support of such schools, and this appropriation shall remain inviolable.

ART. 140. No appropriation shall be made by the General Assembly for the support of any private school or any private institution of learning whatever.

ART. 141. One-half of the funds derived from the poll tax herein provided for shall be appropriated exclusively to the support of the free public schools throughout the State, and the University of New Orleans.

ART. 142. A university shall be established and maintained in the city of New Orleans. It shall be composed of a law, a medical and a collegiate department, each with appropriate faculties. The General Assembly shall provide by law for its organization and maintenance; *Provided*, That all departments of this institution of learning shall be open in common to all students capable of matriculating. No rules or regulations shall be made by the trustees, faculties or other officers of said institution of learning, nor shall any laws be made by the General Assembly violating the letter or spirit of the article under this title.

Art. 143. Institutions for the support of the insane, the education and support of the blind and the deaf and dumb, shall always be fostered by the State, and be subject to such regulations as may be prescribed by the General Assembly.

VI.—UNITED STATES DEPARTMENT OF EDUCATION.

AN ACT TO ESTABLISH A DEPARTMENT OF EDUCATION, APPROVED MARCH 2, 1867.

Section 1. *Be it enacted by the Senate and House of Representatives of the United States of America in Congress assembled,* That there shall be established, at the city of Washington, a department of education, for the purpose of collecting such statistics and facts as shall show the condition and progress of education in the several States and territories, and of diffusing such information respecting the organization and management of schools and school systems and methods of teaching, as shall aid the people of the United States in the establishment and maintenance of efficient school systems; and otherwise promote the cause of education throughout the country.

Sec. 2. *Be it further enacted,* That there shall be appointed by the President, by and with the advice and consent of the Senate, a commissioner of education, who shall be entrusted with the management of the department herein established, and who shall receive a salary of four thousand dollars per annum, and who shall have authority to appoint one chief clerk of his department, who shall receive a salary of two thousand dollars per annum, one clerk who shall receive a salary of eighteen hundred dollars per annum, and one clerk who shall receive a salary of sixteen hundred dollars per annum, which said clerks shall be subject to the appointing and re-moving power of the commissioner of education.

SEC. 3. *Be it further enacted*, That it shall be the duty of the commissioner of education to present annually to Congress a report embodying the results of his investigations and labors, together with a statement of such facts and recommendations as will, in his judgment, subserve the purpose for which this department is established. In the first report made by the commissioner of education under this act, there shall be presented a statement of the several grants of land made by Congress to promote education, and the manner in which the several trusts have been managed; the amount of funds arising therefrom, and the annual proceeds of the same, as far as the same can be determined.

SEC. 4. *Be it further enacted*, That the commissioner of public buildings is hereby authorized and directed to furnish proper offices for the use of the department herein established.

CIRCULAR LETTER BY COMMISSIONER OF EDUCATION.

The undersigned desires to obtain, as early as practicable, accurate but condensed information of the designation, history and present condition of every institution and agency of education in the United States, and of the name, residence and special work of every person in the administration, instruction and management of the same. Any response to this circular in reference to any institution, agency or subject included in the following schedule, addressed to the *Department of Education, Washington, D. C.*, and endorsed "*official*," is entitled, by direction of the Postmaster General, to be conveyed by mail *free* of postage, and will be thankfully received by

 (Signed)   **HENRY BARNARD,**
    Commissioner of Education, Washington, D. C.

SCHEDULE OF INFORMATION SOUGHT RESPECTING SYSTEMS, INSTITUTIONS AND AGENCIES OF EDUCATION.

A—General condition (of district, village, city, county and State). Territorial extent, municipal organization, population, valuation, receipts and expenditures for all public purposes.

B—System of public instruction.

C—Incorporated institutions, and other schools and agencies of education.

I.— Elementary or Primary Education.

(Public, private and denominational, and for boys and girls.)

II.—Academic or Secondary Education.

(Institutions mainly devoted to studies not taught in the elementary schools, and to preparation for college or special schools.)

III.—Collegiate or Superior Education.

(Institutions entitled by law to grant the degree of bachelor of arts or science.)

IV.—Professsional, Special, or Class Education.

(Institutions having special studies and training, such as—1, theology; 2, law; 3, medicine; 4, teaching; 5, agriculture; 6, architecture (design and construction); 7, technology—polytechnic; 8, engineering (civil or mechanical); 9, war (on land or sea); 10, business or trade; 11, navigation; 12, mining and metallurgy; 13, drawing and painting; 14, music; 15, deaf-mutes; 16, blind; 17, idiotic; 18, juvenile offenders; 19, orphans; 20, girls; 21, colored or freedmen; 22, manual or industrial; 23, not specified above—such as chemistry and its applications, modern languages, natural history and geology, steam and its applications, pharmacy, veterinary surgery, etc.)

V.—Supplementary Education.

(1, Sunday and mission schools; 2, apprentice schools; 3, evening schools; 4, courses of lectures; 5, lyceums for debates; 6, reading rooms—periodicals; 7, libraries of reference or circulation; 8, gymnasiums, boat and ball clubs, and other athletic exercises; 9, public gardens, parks and concerts; 10, not specified above.)

VI.—Societies, Institutes, Museums, Cabinets and Galleries for the Advancement of Education, Science, Literature and the Arts.

VII.—Educational and other Periodicals.

VIII.—School Fund and Educational Benefactions.

IX.—Legislation (State or Municipal) respecting Education.

X.—School Architecture.

11

XI.—Penal and Charitable Institutions.

XII.—Churches and other Agencies of Religious Instruction.

XIII.—Reports and other Publications on Schools and Education.

XIV.—Memoirs of teachers and Promoters of Education.

XV.—Examinations (competitive or otherwise) for Admission to National or State Schools, or to Public Service of any kind.

THOMAS W. CONWAY,

Superintendent of Public Education,

State of Louisiana.